How t Knotty

The Essential Guide to Modern Rope Bondage

Morpheous

Green Candy Press

How to Be Knotty
ISBN 978-1-937866-37-2
Published by Green Candy Press
www.greencandypress.com

Copyright © 2017 Morpheous

Printed in Hong Kong by Oceanic Graphic International.
Massively Distributed by P.G.W.

For my beloved wife who believes in me, the dreamer and artist

Contents

Foreword

For as long as I can I can remember, I have been knotty. I was knotty as a youngster. I made knots everywhere—in my hair, with ribbons, with rope, with laces, even bedsheets. It may seem a tad strange that I got so much satisfaction from this, but I could sit for long periods of time binding and unbinding my wrists with rope or a phone cord, all while staring at my partner with a devious, challenging look in my eyes.

The truth is I loved the feeling I got in the pit of my stomach when being tied and bound. My stomach would be in knots, my pussy wet, my heart racing, and all because I knew I was putting myself in the most vulnerable position possible. This is what we do when we become rope bunnies; we allow ourselves to be made vulnerable. And it's this that makes our stomachs flip.

Being tied for me is the ultimate act of love and trust for my partner. It also empowers me and allows me to experience sensations in my body completely free from all worries. As I lay in bed one morning, my partner slowly started to tie my body to our bed using the sheets themselves. I was trying every possible way to get out but I couldn't and I was floored. In that moment, when you know that you are in the hands of someone that can take you to places you've never been before, you have to just let go, and trust that your play partner will take control.

Being submissive requires an amount of trust, and there's no time when trust is more necessary than when playing with rope. Safety is crucial, because it's only when we know we're safe that we can go to our deepest, darkest places—to explore or most perverse and most satisfying desires without worrying about whether or not we're going to get hurt. Back when I was just a newbie knotty girl, I didn't know about safewords and subspace and pressure points. All I wanted was to be tied up.

What I needed, then, was a book like this.

Facing Page: Combining a chest tie with a two-column tie will make leave your sub looking deliciously helpless.

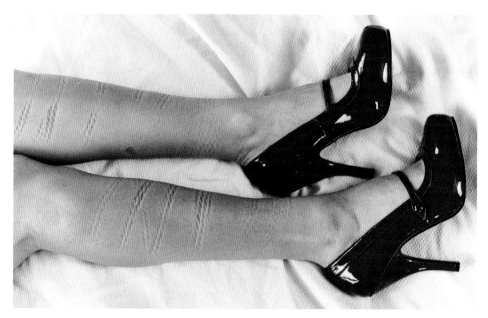

Sexy heels and rope marks: A killer combo in anyone's eyes.

My two female idols growing up were Marilyn Monroe and Bettie Page, and when I first started working in the adult entertainment industry, it was Marilyn and Bettie who influenced me more than anyone else. Marilyn may have been all glamour, but Bettie was the perfect woman to me. She was pretty, sexy, cheeky—and she had the biggest smile on her face when all bound up in rope.

It was Bettie that inspired me to take on my first rope bondage gig, back when I was still Brooke Maschiato and hadn't yet matured into Tera Patrick. On that first bondage shoot, I was tied, tickled, bound and gagged. I was suspended, and I loved it. I wanted more. I was hooked.

Rope quickly became a real part of my life after that. I started to experiment properly with my partners, and found that you never know how turned on you can be until you truly give in to your curiosity. Even today, as I pack to leave for a holiday, I take with me some of my favourite silk corset rope, with a mind to have my partner tie my wrists to the bed, bind my breasts, tether my ankles together and leave me totally at his whim. That sheer, delicious vulnerability is what feeds the fire inside a rope bunny. We love to feel at the mercy of the rope.

It was my rope-obsessed, fervid mind that first led me to Morpheous. When he asked me to participate in his third book, I was ecstatic. I couldn't think of a better way to spend a day than being directed by a bondage master, being tied by his sexy riggers, and being photographed by the wonderful Holly Randall; it was a personal and professional milestone for me.

That day on set with Morpheous, I learned a hell of a lot. Sarah Peaches, Idelsey Love and Bonnie Rotten set the spectacular scene as I arrived for hair and makeup. I was rigged , positioned, and photographed, dividing my time between being the professional model and keeping mental notes on what I could remember to try out later. Morpheous gave firm, eloquent direction the entire time and I can tell you that this is a man who most definitely knows his stuff. When you collaborate with someone whose passion is teaching, there's a particular type of vibe that you get; a tingly sensation that you're being made a true part of something, a moment that's bigger than yourself.

Morpheous and his beautiful ways of executing his passion are displayed here in glorious detail. As you peruse this book I hope you will feel what I felt on set that day—and as you take your own turn to try these ties, I hope that you discover new things just like I did!

The last shot of my day on this project was the gorgeous, incredibly sexy one in which Morpheous bound my breasts. I have always enjoyed breast play; my nipples are so sensitive they can bring me to orgasm (but that's another story altogether). And yet, as the rope wound around my chest in a way I'd never experienced before, I felt sensations that I didn't know existed. It was delicious—and then to see the images days later brought all that intensity right back to me. I had discovered something new, a brand-new pleasure. And I hope you will too.

This book should be a springboard for your next steps into bondage, just like it was for me.

Going further is all part of the beauty and fun, and I hope you take that away from here. Go see a live demonstration, even if you just want to be a voyeur. Please and tease your senses. Whether you watch or participate, you are bound to learn something new about you or the art of tying. I know I have.

Thank you, Morpheous, for inviting me into your world. Like your readers, I'll take away knowledge, passion and experience from this book, and I know I'll never quite be the same again.

Stay knotty!

—Tera Patrick

Preface

I've had the pleasure of shooting multiple bondage books for Lord Morpheous, and I have to say that this volume is one of my favorites.

I have always had a personal affinity with kink (especially bondage!) so this was a wonderful project to work on. When Morpheous contacted me about this book, I couldn't say yes fast enough. *How to be Knotty* combines my two favorite things: Beautiful glamour photography and the kinky flavor of S&M bondage. The way that Morpheous combines the visceral excitement of being restrained with the visual beauty of his intricate rope work is truly astounding. I love how he embraces the classic glamour aesthetic with a wicked twist; this contrast of glamour and kink makes for a truly intoxicating image.

He has worked with some wonderful models in this book: Mosh, Ana Foxx, Vanessa Lake, Samantha Saint, Candleboxxx, Odette, Samantha Rone and Jayden Jaymes, to name a few. So many names from so many different corners of the world of erotic entertainment. Who knew that you could actually create an entire outfit out of rope? Check out Samantha and Mosh's outfits in this book if you don't believe such a thing is possible!

Morpheous' dedication to his work, his attention to detail and his affinity with the S&M lifestyle really come through in this book. More than ever, his personality is present in his work. He is knowledgeable, patient and is always attentive to his subject's needs and comfort, and you can see this in the resulting images.

Working with Morpheous is a fantastic experience thanks to the creative freedom he allows, but for me it has also been quite the education. Anyone who is interested in learning the art of rope bondage should definitely get this book—you (and your partner) will be happy you did!

—Holly

Facing Page: This book will have you making your own intricate rope pieces, just like this one.

For the Love of Rope

We all have passions in life. Yours might be food, or fishing, or the movies of John Waters. As most people know, mine is rope.

Whether or not you've read my previous books *How to Be Kinky: A Beginner's Guide to BDSM*, *How to be Kinkier: More Adventures in Adult Playtime* and *Bondage Basics: Naughty Knots and Risqué Restraints You Need To Know*, it should be fairly clear to you by now that, although my local hardware store does know me fairly well, the dozens of coiled ropes in my garage aren't used to secure things to the top of my car. My rope passion doesn't involve climbing, or abseiling down buildings, or even getting neck deep in water with only a flashlight to light my way (although things certainly do get a bit wet).

My rope passion involves quickened breath, and marks left on skin, and the distinct noise of someone squeaking and writhing in a barely concealed orgasm. It involves fast hands weaving beautiful patterns around warm bodies, with torsos and limbs bent into unnatural positions leaving their owners feeling deliciously vulnerable. The only exploring I do is to let my hands orient themselves around the soft and supple flesh of my rope bunnies. In short, my passion is tying up sexy folks.

As you're reading this book, I'll assume that you know what I'm talking about. You too know the hedonistic pleasure of being suspended in a complex body harness, or stroking the skin of your submissive while you contort them in ways that will leave them totally at your mercy. You've spent hours rubbing Arnica cream into skin burns after a long night's play, and

Facing Page: Seeing a sub in their fluffy headspace makes any rigger weak at the knees.

you've stroked the hair of an exhausted and exhilarated bunny after a particularly intense session. You, like me, think about rope before you go to bed and when you wake up in the morning. Whether you're a rigger, a bunny or simply a bondage aficionado who likes to look from the sidelines, you know the sensual pleasure that rope can bring.

This book, then, is for you.

It's for those who've played with rope before, and those who've grown beyond what beginner bondage books can teach them. This book is meant to bring you even further inside the inner sanctum, the community of folks who love nothing more than tying each other up on a rainy Friday night; those who wander around Home Depot like everyone else on the weekends but who are buying hardware for very different reasons.

This one is for the perverts.

I've been lucky enough to teach rope bondage classes all over the world, to students at all levels of skill. There's nothing quite like watching a student practice what you've taught them, master it, then turn it into something wholly new and inspired. This is what I'm aiming to achieve with this book. Whether you're interested in enhancing your bondage skills for the sheer love of the art form, or to use in your bedroom, dungeon or anywhere else you can get away with it, in these pages you'll learn new knots and ties that are a little more difficult than you'll find in beginner rope bondage books. I'll trust that you've read one of my previous books and that you've practiced the basics until you know them like the back of your hand. I'll assume that you've got your basic stuff down and are eager to learn more. I'll show you the sort of "building block" knots that will allow you to go far beyond the scope of this book, putting together new combinations and inspired pairings that make up whole new harnesses, body ties and everything else besides. This book is intended as a springboard; you'll need it to make the jump, but you'll get way further once you've used it.

This book will teach you how to tie for purposes of both sex and art, although of course the two can be and often are intertwined (much like the limbs of your delicious muse). Express your creativity in bringing these two areas together. There's nothing more artistic than a butt-naked sub

Facing Page: Traditional rope textures can make for an incredible experience for your bunny.

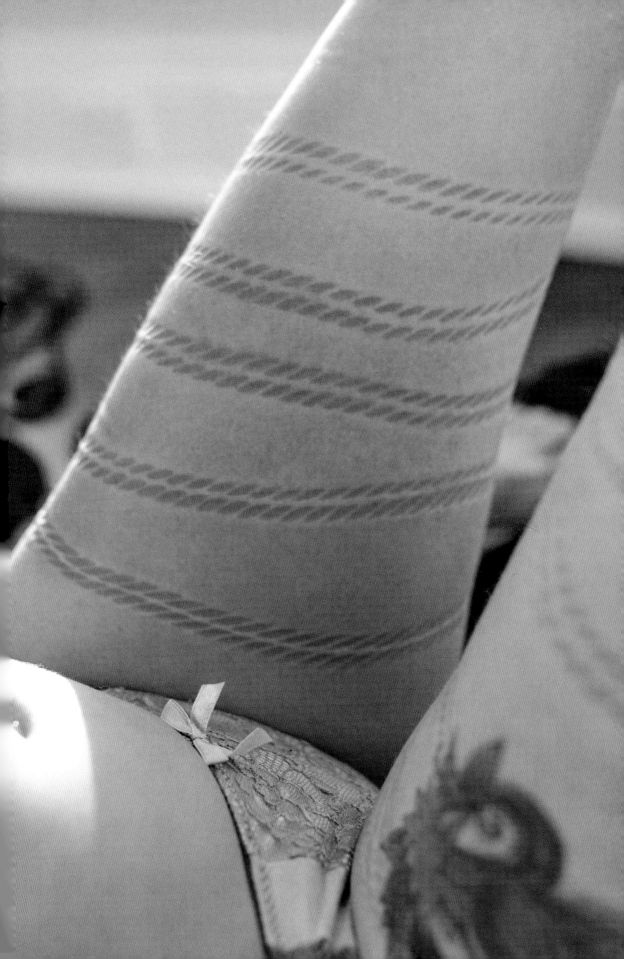

trussed up like a Christmas turkey, basking in the soft light streaming in through your studio window (which is exactly why I always have my camera on hand).

Modern bondage has both art and eroticism in its history. To understand this, one has to look to its origins. My style of rope work, like that of the many other passionate and talented riggers working around the world today, is very much part of the movement over the last decade or so that has brought together both Eastern and Western bondage styles in a contemporary fusion. Like a burrito stuffed with noodles and Kung Pao chicken, or a California sushi roll packed with avocado, modern rope bondage takes the best of the East and the best of the West and marries them in a delectable, sexy little package that's totally irresistible.

The origins and long history of Eastern rope bondage are well known in the bondage community. It's generally accepted that the Japanese practice of Hojojutsu, a fascinating martial art whose practitioners, mainly Samurai, restrained people using rope, is the seed from which the Eastern school of bondage grew (and grew, and grew…). Rope art eventually found its way in Japan's kabuki theatre, a mixture of dance and drama that's nothing if not elaborate, and this spurred rope art into mainstream popularity during the Edo period of the early 1800s. This rope art was called "kinbaku" and brought together the artistic and physical aspects of rope bondage with a new, sexual side. And we're lucky that it did!

The incredible Japanese artist Seiu Ito is credited as being the catalyst for kinbaku's huge popularity, as his kinbaku paintings helped spread interest for the practice all over the world—and, in fact, his paintings are still a huge inspiration for kinksters and artists today. The 1950s saw another spurt of popularity for Ito's work, and this led to the fusion of kinbaku with the more aesthetic Western style to form shibari, kinbaku's more artistic cousin. Shibari remains the most popular Eastern-inspired rope bondage style today, with many practitioners all over the world.

The Western rope bondage style, however, has something of a darker origin. The first mention of bondage in the West appears in a 13th Century epic Austrian poem called the Nibelungenlied, in which the Warrior Queen of Iceland is bound and raped by two men, including her husband,

Facing Page: Make sure your sub is comfortable, and their circulation is good, even in more difficult poses.

after which she is shorn of her strength and is submissive to her husband for the rest of her life. Hardly a great start. However, in the early 1900s, an Englishman named John Willie founded and published *Bizarre Magazine* to introduce the world to his own personal fetish: Rope bondage (hopefully not inspired by the Nibelungenlied). Willie's erotic artworks, featuring pinup girls in ropes and chains and looking thoroughly and sexily vulnerable, brought the idea of sexual binding and restraint to a thirsty Western world.

This surge of popularity continued into the 1940s when Peruvian painter and kinkster Alberto Vargas grabbed the sensuality of Willie's work and turbocharged it. The Vargas Girls series of paintings showed pinup girls joyfully clad in body stockings, high-cut dresses and sometimes only gloves, wielding whips and role-playing with giddy abandon. The Vargas Girls were having a grand ol' time, and people loved them. Almost all pinup art and photography today is inspired by Alberto Vargas, and kink photography and practice is undoubtedly influenced by him too.

Of course, no discussion of bondage popularity in the Western world can be complete without a mention of the phenomenal Bettie Page. The single most identifiable face in the world of kink, art and bondage, Bettie was catapulted into popularity by American photographer Irving Klaw, who had his models pose for fetish photos which were then sold through mail orders. Long black gloves, stocking, whips, ball gags; Bettie posed like a BDSM queen and was loved as such too—especially by the "special clientele" for which Bettie starred in Klaw-directed films catering directly to the requests of the client. Though silent, these films showed females engaging in a wide variety of BDSM scenarios, including bondage, restraining and gagging; in fact, the most famous still image from these films shows Bettie herself gagged and tied up in a web of ropes. Not only did Bettie follow the Vargas Girls in looking like she was having the time of her life, but she was also tied up and bound mostly by Klaw's sister, the first woman to famously engage in bondage with another woman. Since the '50s, Bettie Page has remained an enduring symbol of gleeful sexuality and BDSM tendencies, and it's hard to find a kinkster today who wasn't enjoyed some sinful thoughts about Bettie in the middle of a scene.

This Western love of the bondage pinup style and the joy of female agency when it comes to sex have, in recent years, been infused with the artistic shibari style and the more sexual kinbaku practice to create some-

Traditional rope in the hands of a master can do magical things.

thing altogether more fascinating than either one. Modern rope bondage is a delicious blend of centuries of rope work and filthy behavior, with a good dash of style and pleasure thrown in for good measure.

And so, we come to my own modern rope bondage. As you'll see within these pages, there's nothing I love more than letting my creativity fly with bright rope and supple flesh, combining ties and knots to make something brand new but still classic, and to shoot models with style and panache while they're all trussed up like turkeys. I love giving others the tools to explore their sexuality through modern bondage, whether that's in the privacy of their own bedroom or in the smoky, sensual atmosphere of a bondage exhibition night or a filthy little sex club. Whatever you love rope for, it's my job to teach you how to do it well, and do it right—and how to keep getting better and better.

So let's get right on with it.

Chapter One

Beyond the Beginnings

This is not a beginner rope bondage book. There are some incredible rope bondage books aimed at total newbies, and all three of my previous books cover simple bondage to a greater or lesser extent. I suggest that you immerse yourself in these titles and ensure that you have the basics of bondage down before you approach any of the ties in this book. Practice, practice and practice again.

What's that? You've read them?

Then let's talk about what comes next.

In my previous books, I've laid the foundations for what comes here; for you, the reader, to pick up the ball and run to the end zone with it. Once you've learned the basics of bondage, this book opens up the opportunity for more artistic expression, to get your creative juices flowing. As with any art form, the job of the teacher is to pass on the tools that the student needs, and then to inspire them to use those tools (insert salacious tool joke here). A piano teacher may force her student to repeat scales and arpeggios by heart, then to study minims and semibreves until they can read any new piece of music by sight, but at some point, the role of the teacher changes; she can only sit back and let the creative skill of her student fly, dipping in only when she is needed.

In this book, there are a lot of new things to learn. The complexity of the ties will be greater than what you're used to. Learn the ties, practice them, and once you have them perfect, use my versions of them as a point of departure to start experimenting with making your own ties. Start with

Facing Page: This book takes you beyond the basics of bondage and closer to work like this.

one little addition here or there, or a slight change to the basic version, perhaps adding something you've seen on different pages, or adding two things together to make one larger tie. Once you're confident with the knots, play around with them, and with your submissive; experiment with your creativity and let yourself be inspired.

My previous books are your scales and arpeggios. The ties in this book are your minims and semibreves. At the end of this book, I want to sit back while you take these tools and make something new with them. I want to watch you fly.

Of course, like anything else, your progression with rope bondage depends on how much you practice. In order to become a serious rigger, you need to put in the hours that it takes to get better and better. Like a pianist, you should be able to keep playing without even looking at what you're doing; working your hands should become second nature, allowing you to focus on the passion of the piece. As a smart music teacher once said, practice makes permanent: Don't keep going until you get it right, keep going until you can't get it wrong.

After all—the practice is pretty fun.

When moving past beginner bondage and on to more intricate and more complex ties, the biggest challenge is allowing yourself to experiment. When someone's safety quite literally hangs in the balance, it can be difficult to take that step; to trust yourself and your knowledge enough to create something totally brand new. To be wary of this is a good sign; it shows that you're aware of your responsibilities when playing with rope, and that the health and safety of (all) your play partners is at the forefront of your mind. Good little rigger; you've learned well. However, you should (and will) proceed with caution; go slow, be gentle, and check in with your sub often and clearly—but do take that step. If anything goes wrong, you'll have your safety shears to hand and your aftercare kit ready. You're ready, young Padawan. I believe in you.

The key to becoming a master of anything is learning the basics by heart and still being excited to experiment. This is true of rope bondage, whether you're a rigger or a rope bunny.

Becoming a Better Bunny

So you want to be tied up in delicious ways and have already had a chance to try out being tied from my other books? Good for you! I'm

It's all about attitude. If you're not having a fantastic time, then you're doing it wrong.

happy to help. No, no—don't thank me. Seriously, it's my pleasure. If you had as much of a good time as I imagine you did, I guess you're wondering what you can do to ensure that your further exploration into rope will be as enjoyable as it can be. I'm glad you're considering this. Some people don't.

Intermediate rope bondage poses a new and fresh set of challenges whether you're the one bound up in rope or the one doing the binding. It's not just the rigger that has to put work into progressing; the bunny does too.

It's important to note that the strength, stamina and mental fitness of a rope bunny is absolutely crucial when moving forward into more intense ties and binds. Rope bunnies are like athletes; they push their bodies beyond the norm, stretching their physical and mental agility to produce phenomenal results. They need to know every part of their bodies and how each one feels from the inside out, so that when something is "off," they can respond immediately. If they want to be used as putty from which beautiful artwork can be made, they need to be supple and healthy and able to stretch. They need to ensure they're emotionally ready for ties

3

that cover more of their bodies and hold them in more constrictive positions. They need to train.

As a rope bunny, you need to ensure that you are fit, in all ways, for the challenge ahead of you. Do you work out or do yoga? Do you go to Pilates classes, run, swim or walk often? To get more out of rope bondage, which is just as much a physical experience as mental, you will have a better time if you are used to stretching, moving and feeling good and healthy. Of course, we're not saying here that you need to be any particular body shape or size; I hope that I've shown throughout my books that the rope bondage community is wide and diverse. You don't need to have bulging muscles to be wrapped up in rope, nor to have the "perfect" body. I don't advocate anyone being obsessed with the gym, but rather looking after themselves to ensure that playtime is safe and fun. When it comes to fitness, every little bit helps to keep your joints limber, your back flexible and your focus sharp enough to know your body when something isn't "right."

This goes for your mental state as much as your physical self. Bondage is emotionally strenuous, and as you already know, when you fly high, you have to expect to come down to earth. Bondage brings about so many ups and downs that it's important to invest in your baseline; ensure that you're as emotionally stable as you can be, so that when you deviate from that baseline, you've got something solid to come back to. You should also be strong enough not to force yourself into play if you're not feeling absolutely perfect about it. Sometimes you might be totally jazzed about playing with rope. You might have looked forward to it all week, getting embarrassingly wet at work while thinking about the knots pressing against your skin, about the feel of your master's hands on your body as you hang in a harness made just for you. You have been longing for your play session and can't wait to get started. Then, on the night of your rope date, something is off. You don't feel quite as excited as you should be; you're light-headed or anxious, and the connection with your rigger doesn't feel like it usually does. It could be something physical, or something emotional, or something that you can't put your finger on at all; it doesn't matter. It's okay to tell your partner that something isn't "right" and you want to reschedule. Perhaps you can just cuddle that night instead? Sure,

Facing Page: Yoga, pilates and even basic aerobics can be super beneficial for a bunny—and a rigger too!

it can be disappointing to you or your rigger but anyone worth their salt who respects you should honor that and not pressure you into play. This is supposed to be fun; we call it "play" for a reason!

However, when you move into intermediate rope bondage as a bunny, it's not just all about you. As your rigger learns and masters more complex knots and ties, you should learn about them too. If you understand what a certain tie does to your body, you'll be better placed to enjoy the sensation, not to mention more informed about what you should and shouldn't feel when a knot is in place. As we've discussed before in previous books, the well-being of all participants in a play session is in the hands of all the other participants; you should know what you're getting into just as much as the rigger does. Learn along with your play partner and it will bring you together too; there's nothing as sexy as a massive mind.

Many rope bunnies find themselves more interested in becoming riggers as they move further into more intricate and difficult bondage, I suppose in the same way that actors find themselves interested in directing, and musicians tend towards becoming producers as their careers progress. If rope is part of a D/s relationship you have, this can be helpful as you can Top others for the pleasure of your Dom, or can switch the roles up a little as and when the fancy takes you. Event the most hardcore Master or Mistress likes to have the power taken away from them now and again. You also might want to introduce other play partners into your dynamic, some of whom will also be submissive. In this case, your Dom can train you up in the basics of bondage so that you can play Dom to your new submissive partner. Passing on your knowledge to another person and watching them flourish is incredibly sexy, and helps to build an even greater bond between you. Personally, I like nothing more than watching one of my submissives tie up one of my other subs, using ties and techniques that I've taught her through hours of play. Having a submissive play Top for your pleasure is super attractive; there's nothing hotter than someone who isn't afraid to take control!

If this isn't your path, don't worry; you don't have to move behind the camera, as it were, to engage in rope bondage further. But if you want to—well, if Madonna can direct a movie, so can you.

Facing Page: A bunny should be in tune with their body, and should feel comfortable saying if something doesn't feel quite right.

Becoming a Better Rigger

So. You've already acquired some basic bondage skills and now you're like a dog with a bone(r). You can't let go. It's all you think about. You're desperate to learn more. Well you've come to the right place.

But wait.

You may have seen some delicious "super bondage" online and picked up this book so you can try it out for yourself. I can understand that; those luscious, sexually charged images of beautiful bodies bent and twisted and folded and turned into exquisite shapes are enough to have any passionate rigger reaching for their rope. However, what isn't conveyed through the internet is the time, man-hours and skill invested into making those photos. Professional pictures usually have a moderately sized team of skilled people creating them. Here's what you don't see: The photographer, the lighting tech, the rigger or riggers and their many assistants. Making bondage look this perfect is a big job. In this book I have had the help of a fantastic team of riggers and assistants to make the images lush, sexy and safe.

It's important to remember the reality, however. The reality is hard work, and practice, and considering the safety of a tie above how good it looks—every single time. Safety is always my primary concern. Always. We make it look easy in order for you to be inspired.

I fully applaud you in your decision to go further into rope bondage. I hope, like me, that you find a greater sense of fulfillment and the purest type of joy from becoming a bona fide rope obsessive. However, move forward with the knowledge that you, as a rigger, shoulder a lot of responsibility. We've talked about responsibility a lot in my previous books, and your duty to your submissives, your play partners and yourself grows exponentially as you move into more intermediate and eventually expert-level rope bondage. Just because you've mastered the basics, this doesn't mean that you can start taking risks in order to achieve the sort of results you can see online and in books. If anything, you should become more risk-averse, less focused on the final look of a tie and more on the connection you have with your partner/s. The true zenith of bondage is when the electricity between partners is palpable; when there's sweat in the air, and

Facing Page: As a rigger, you should be strong enough to ensure the physical safety of anyone you're playing with.

marks on skin, and every single movement is charged. These scenes are rarely that photogenic—but then, real hot sex doesn't look that good on camera either.

If you are interested in furthering your photography skills and recreating scenes like the ones in this book, I fully support you. But remember that you've got to learn to do all of this before you can learn to make it look great. Be careful and go slow at first; there is no need to rush. When you've mastered the ties shown in this book, I fully encourage you to seek out personalized instruction to take you beyond what the printed page can teach you. Come to one of my workshops, take a course in your local area, or find a mentor within your local community. All these things will allow you to nurture your skills and grow as both a rigger and a person—and to become a truly great professional in the rope bondage community.

We've already talked in this chapter about the importance of a rope bunny being fit and healthy. But wait—you don't get off the hook with this either, buddy. Your mental and physical well-being should be of primary importance to you as you explore further into rope. It's not just a bunny that experiences the emotional highs and lows of bondage; you do too. Playtime brings highs for everyone, and you need to be of sufficient mental fitness to be able to support your bunny or bunnies in their emotional recovery as well as dealing with your own inevitable "lows" too. You should also be ready for the physical strain that difficult bondage will place on you; if you're going to place your submissives into full body harnesses that restrict their movement entirely, you should be of adequate strength to shift them and turn them, should they find themselves in an uncomfortable or dangerous position. If you're going to weave gorgeous full-body ties around your play partners and then suspend them from the rafters, you need to be strong enough to hoist them skywards—and keep them there safely. If you seek to take away someone's ability to physically support themselves, you should have enough strength to do it for them. Don't forget this, and never suspend someone that you're not strong enough to support. Make sure, too, that you have the skills and knowledge sufficient to help someone who may be having a medical emergency; such situations are rare, but it's your duty to prepare yourself just in case. Learn anatomy.

Facing Page: Never lift someone whose weight you can't safely bear. Your responsibility as the rigger is to everyone's well-being.

11

Learn safety. Take first aid lessons just to stay current. There is no substitute for experience. Remember: The responsibility is yours.

This book is meant to allow you to gain skills and be inspired; it isn't an excuse for you to recreate the ties if you don't pay attention to safety. Listen to your rope bunny, connect with them and value them. Do it right and you will play again and again. Do it wrong and you'll never get a second chance. The rope is important but the connection with and safety of your partner is more so.

Respecting the Art Form

We join a rich history when we decide to tie each other up. As we discussed in the introduction to this book, the roots of rope bondage are fascinating and varied. Whether you're practicing bondage privately at home or you're an active part of the rigging community in your area, you're part of a tradition that goes back centuries, and will stretch on for much longer than any of us will. For this reason, it's important to practice bondage with something approaching reverence for the art form itself. I'm not saying you need to build a shrine to Seiu Ito or anything (although it's not my place to tell you how to decorate your home; knit a life-size homage to Bettie Page if you want to), but what I am saying is that it's worth respecting bondage not only because of the intensity of the experience but because of the skill, creativity and passion of those who've come before you (pun absolutely intended).

To this end, I'd always encourage you to reach out to and support other riggers working in your local community. I personally believe that munches (sex-free gatherings of like-minded kinky folk) are a great way to get out there and find inspiration from your peers, but even if you're not into that, there are most likely bondage shows and events around that you will be comfortable attending. Here you can see the work of others and support their creativity, and you'll no doubt find tips and tricks that you can assimilate into your practice too. The bondage community has always been an interwoven one, with people sharing ties and methods and encouraging experimentation; be a part of this if you can. My rope bondage exhibition event, Morpheous' Rope Bondage Extravaganza, has grown up from a single-city event once a year to a global movement, with events happening on every continent except Antarctica, precisely because bondage is something that is to be shared. Come out to one of our bondage exhibition events; you won't regret it!

The connection between the rigger and the bunny is the most important thing.
Never lose sight of that.

Prerequisite Knowledge

The ties in this book build upon those shown in my first three books,
How to Be Kinky: A Beginner's Guide to BDSM, *How to be Kinkier: More
Adventures in Adult Playtime* and *Bondage Basics: Naughty Knots and Risqué
Restraints You Need To Know*. I highly recommend that you get these
books, or any of the ones listed in the resources section at the end of this
book, read them cover to cover, scribble notes in them, learn them inside
out and then start on this one.

These books show you the basic ties, knots and general knowledge that
we'll be utilizing in this book. I'm going to assume a level of prior knowledge here; in fact, I'm going to assume that you've read my previous
books. I'll use bondage terminology and refer to basic knots and talk
about safety in a way that should already make sense to you. If it doesn't,
you're not ready for this book.

I'll also be using ties you should have learned already, like the cuff tie
or the two-handed parallel tie. If there's anything that I haven't explained
here, it's because it has been explained in my previous books. Don't worry;
I won't introduce anything that's not fully illustrated somewhere else.

You should already know about basic bondage safety and have a safety kit stocked and by your side, ready for use. You should know about nerve locations, and sub drop, and aftercare, and how exactly to check that someone's circulation is adequate. You should know what cream to use to get rid of bruises and marks, and what to do if there are abrasions on someone's skin.

You should have working knowledge of things like limb restraints, hogties, simple decorative ties, nerve locations, rope extension, the square knot, the belt lock and the corset tie. You should be confident in your ability to communicate effectively with your partner, knowing their body language as well as their body. Are they grunting and groaning in the wrong way? Are they trying too hard to endure a bad kind of pain because they don't want to disappoint you? As the rigger, you need to know they will be forthcoming with the information, either verbal or non.

The better prepared you are for anything, the more confident you can feel.

Further Education

I'm thrilled that you've picked me as your tutor through intermediate bondage. Honestly, I'm flattered. I mean, don't get me flowers or anything, but it means a lot. I have learned a lot over the past twenty years and I hope that you too will someday be in a place where you can pass on your knowledge in a positive and helpful way to those new when the time comes.

The ties in this book are split into three chapters and set in order of difficulty to ensure that you work from easiest to most challenging. This is the safest way to progress here, and I encourage you to make sure you're confident and comfortable in the easier ties before moving on. I've hosted many rope bondage workshops and classes over the years, including the world's largest bondage event, Morpheous' Bondage Extravaganza, and I always make sure to impress this upon my students: There is no rush. This is not a race. You won't be taking a test at the end and you certainly won't be getting any flashy certificates; bondage is a journey, not a rush to a destination. By choosing to progress into further bondage with your partner(s), you're embarking on an intense and personal journey with them. Respect each other and put time aside to properly practice and then to look after each other; aftercare is important, checking in with their

Facing Page: Colored rope and some sexy shoes always bring a glamour to a play session.

emotional needs is important, giving yourself the space to learn is important. Take your time and enjoy the process of learning. There's a reason we've used sexy, incredibly attractive models in this book—because I want you to take your time and enjoy reading it!

But what cums (sorry) after that? What happens when you've mastered all the ties in this book and are still looking for more?

Well—now the world's your oyster! Use this book as a starting point for exploring real-life bondage lessons. There are more and more opportunities to study in person than ever before. There are many bondage workshops and classes taught by fantastic riggers, and there are likely to be a few of these in your local area. Such workshops will allow you to progress even further, but this time under the care and instruction of a professional who's right there with you. I'd also highly recommend finding a mentor from the bondage community; a person who you can respect and learn from and who is willing to teach you. There's nothing better than one-to-one tuition, and as integrity is so important in the BDSM world, your mentor should be someone who is the epitome of everything the kink community aspires to. They should be communicative, nurturing, honest and polite. They should be caring and compassionate, and should contribute to the well-being of the partners that they play with. Choose a mentor that inspires you to be the best person you can be, both in and out of the bondage world. With a mentor like this, you'll go far.

As someone who has taught many classes in kink and rope bondage over the years, I encourage you to never leave the path of learning. I am always constantly learning and am humbled by those that have come before me and those that I inspire going forward. The fusion style that I'll teach you in this book allows us to reach into our own creativity; it's because of this style that rope bondage has grown in ways never before thought possible. The best path forward is the one on which we break free of old boundaries but at the same time honor the traditions that have laid the groundwork on which we can grow. If you are impressed by the photos and knots and wraps and passion in this book, know that I stand on the shoulders of giants and that as the torch passes from generation to generation, you add a link in the chain of experience. Do so with honor. Respect the craft.

Facing Page: A rope bunny in her native environment: swaddled in rope, having the time of her life.

Chapter Two

Safety, Safety and Still More Safety

Would you go snowboarding without a helmet? Would you drive without a seat belt? Would you go scuba diving without an air tank?

Of course you wouldn't. Especially not the scuba diving.

When we're doing anything that involves risk, we need to take steps to keep ourselves, and others, safe. This is especially true when we're exploring rope bondage. But of course, you know all this. A discussion about safety is the very first class of Bondage 101, and you wouldn't have gotten this far into the kink world if you didn't play nice.

However, it's easy to be drawn into a false sense of security (no pun intended) about safety if you've been exploring rope bondage for a long time—or even for a relatively short time. The rules that we adhere to so strictly in our first month or so can begin to seem a little unnecessary after a year or so of perfect play, when no one's fingers have ever turned blue and none of your bunnies have ever discovered an emotional trigger that they didn't know they had. However, to go back to our driving analogy, even if you've been driving all your life and never had an accident, does that mean you should stop wearing your seat belt? And do you really want to take that risk?

Whether you've been involved with rope bondage for one year, ten years or sixty years, safety should be at the forefront of your mind

Facing Page: When ties become this intricate, it's important to have shears close by. You should be able to remove someone from rope in seconds.

through every play session, from beginning to end. When we move from beginner rope play to intermediate rope play, the risks—and so the responsibilities—become that much greater.

A conversation about safety in rope bondage can be endless, so I'll only truly be touching the surface in this chapter; it's a refresher, as it were, on things you should already know. However, if you're dedicated to growing in and with rope bondage, I highly recommend *On the Safe Edge* by Trevor Jacques, which is a seminal book on the subject of bondage safety. Essays and books on this subject are essential reading for any rigger or rope bunny looking to move further into the discipline. I've also covered the subject of safety extensively in my other books, so read the relevant chapters in those books to widen your knowledge too.

It should go without saying, but no matter how much you've read and how much experience you have, you should never push the envelope in an emergency situation. For any serious occurrences or health issues, seek the advice of a medical professional immediately and without delay. You might feel stupid calling an ambulance while you're top to toe in leather, but the health of everyone concerned is much more important than pride. And hey—maybe the paramedics will be secret perverts too!

Consent

Consent is key—always and in every single situation.

The joy of bondage and of kinky sex more generally lies in the ability to give oneself up totally to another, whether that's for two minutes, an hour, or an entire evening. The joy of being a Dom is to have a submissive or a rope bunny place themselves quite literally in your hands, giving themselves over to you. None of this is possible unless consent is consistently sought and consistently given—only when you can be totally sure that your partner is agreeing to everything you're doing can you both revel in the pleasure of it.

Consent is defined as "positive, unambiguous, and voluntary agreement to engage in specific sexual activity throughout a sexual encounter".[1]

1. http://smr.yale.edu/yale-sexual-misconduct-policies-and-related-definitions

Facing Page: Don't get too distracted by how great your submissive looks; safety should always be at the front of your mind.

Someone has not given consent if they simply haven't said no. Consent is positively saying "yes" in sound mind.

This, of course, applies to both (or all) participants in any and every scene. It should also be noted that consent does not have any time frame; it can be withdrawn immediately and at any point.

It doesn't matter whether your sub or your rigger has expressed willingness all the way through the event only to change their minds and say no; when they say no, they mean no. For the purposes of safety, you should also assume that when they stop saying "yes," they mean no. Perhaps something has progressed further than they expected, or perhaps they're experiencing negative emotions that have been brought up by the situation. Perhaps they're simply tired or uncomfortable. The reasons don't matter; what matters is that once consent is withdrawn, or if a participant has become unable to express their affirmative agreement, the event must stop. Only "yes" means "yes."

Of course, part of kink is saying no when really, we mean yes; to beg for something to be over when we desperately want it to continue. Role-playing, teasing and play coercion are all popular games that we play, especially with bondage, meaning that no doesn't always mean no. For this reason, many kinksters employ a traffic light system to ensure that consent and well-being are maintained: Green means yes, or keep going, yellow means that something about the situation should be changed or given some attention, and red means stop immediately. Red makes a great safeword regardless of the situation; it is a very obvious and easily spoken statement of non-consent.

Of course, you can get creative, using whatever words you find easy to use. If you don't use words that are common to you, you risk hesitation in their use, but if you prefer to use "blancmange" as your safeword, then so be it.

If you just love having your mouth stuffed with a ball gag or your own dirty panties while you're hanging prone in a beautiful rope harness, then you may not always be able to say red or green, or yes or no, or even blancmange if a scene starts to go beyond what you imagined. In such an instance, make sure that your Dom has placed something heavy in your

Facing Page: Check in with your sub. Check for consent. A smile is great but only "yes" means "yes."

hands before the scene begins. Ensure that you're in such a position that you can drop that something to the ground and make a sound. If you become uncomfortable in any way, you can drop the objects and alert your Dom to the fact that you want the play to stop. When playing with rope, heavy objects serve a dual function; if a tie is too tight and a submissive's hands can no longer grip, then the objects will fall to the floor, clatter and alert other participants of the need of immediate action.

Mental Well-Being

It should go without saying that before entering into any bondage scene with a new partner, you should be aware of any mental health issues that they might have, and you should have a frank and honest discussion with that person about your own. Bondage is as emotional as it is physical, and in the same way that you need to know about your partner's dodgy knee from a football injury in high school, you need to know if they hate the word "slut" or have negative experiences with a certain type of language.

It's imperative to create a tone of respect in every bondage scene; use "I" language and never use terms that blame any partner in the scene. If you need to give direction, be sure to do so in a positive, affirmative way that explains why the movement needs to happen and what you're going to do once it's there. Create safe parameters and stick to them; they will help you to truly give yourselves over to each other and let go in that way that only BDSM allows.

Check in with your sub often; a simple "How are you doing in there, sweetheart?" with a gentle stroke of an exposed body part can allow your bunny to express any discomfort, and therefore you can ensure that all participants are having their needs met and are as comfortable as possible. Being restrained can bring about heightened emotions, so keep your language as gentle as your touch and always ensure that your sub feels appreciated, respected and looked after. Explain what you're doing and why: For instance, "I'm going to pull your leg in towards you so I can better expose you to pleasure you," is a better direction than "Pull your leg in." We all enjoy positive feedback, so be a good boss!

It should go without saying at this point that aftercare is not only necessary but should be considered as important as the scene itself. Untie your sub sensually and slowly; allow him to come back to the feeling of freedom without plunging him into it too quickly. Caress and reassure;

Before you start playing, make sure you know all your sub's potential triggers and hard boundaries.

tell him that he's been a good boy, tell him that he's amazing, that he's incredible, massage each limb as you unbind it. Create a comforting, low-light area for your sub to relax in after they've been untied, and rub Arnica cream into any area that might have become a little tender. Ensure that any rope abrasions (they can happen) are dealt with and kept clean, and tell your sub often how much you enjoyed tying them and how beautiful they are. Some people find that "vanilla" sexual activities or even just sensual massage can help them to come down from a scene, but this needs to be discussed beforehand and must always be agreed upon by both parties. Subs will feel vulnerable after a scene, so keep in mind that any sexual activities should make them feel satisfied and appreciated.

Aftercare is a space we create to allow partners to talk about their experience honestly, and to allow the power dynamics to soften back into the normal, everyday dynamic that the participants enjoy. For this reason, all parties involved should be allowed come back to their normal selves in as much time as they need, with whatever level of assistance they need. Ask questions about your sub's experience and talk about yours. Be honest about what you enjoyed and what you'd like to do more of in future;

don't speak negatively about things that you didn't enjoy so much, but simply focus on other parts of the experience. Pleasant music, favorite movies or comedy shows, comforting foods, maybe even reading a book to your sub—all these things will make for a very happy, very supporting aftercare session that leaves everyone feeling fantastic and appreciated, and keen to go back for more!

Sub Drop and Top Drop

It may be that as your bondage sessions become more complex and intense, your rope bunny will become overwhelmed and experience sub drop after a particularly emotional scene. The rigger, too, might experience a similar condition known as top drop.

When in a scene, the submissive partner is drawn to focus more greatly on the physical aspects; feeling pain or restraint becomes the significant experience in that moment, and this can allow the sub to move into a trancelike mental space, the physicality letting the mind become still and focused. When faced with pain or stressful situations, the body can release endorphins as well as a whole heap of other neurochemicals like enkephalins, dopamine and oxytocin. The latter groups are the body's natural painkillers, which act very much like morphine. These chemicals, combined with the trancelike state above, can allow submissives to enter into what's known as "subspace," the drugged-like, otherworldly state that most bondage fans dream of. In subspace, the world outside the scene ceases to exist; dopamine floods the brain much like when a person is on drugs, and this makes everything else fall away leaving just the scene and the people in it. When your submissive enters this state, he or she may be unable to respond to your questioning; when your submissive cannot express their feelings because they are deep into subspace, consider ending the scene slowly. You should know your partner well enough to know their reactions to subspace, but it's better to be safe than sorry.

Subspace is a glorious thing to experience. However, as the old adage goes, what goes up must come down. Dopamine is the body's response to endorphins (or orgasm), and it is released quickly and in a big way. That

Facing Page: Facedown, ass up is everyone's favorite position—but you should get consistent feedback from your bunny that she's comfortable and feeling great.

dopamine, unfortunately, doesn't hang around, and another neurochemical known as prolactin is released as the levels of dopamine drop. Prolactin is the hormone that's more accurately described as a stress chemical, and it can make the individual feel alienated, quiet, confused and depressed. It is this that can cause sub drop in the hours or days after a particularly intense scene.

However, it's not only the submissive partners that can experience this drop in dopamine. Tops and riggers can also suffer from these negative feelings after their own dopamine levels drop off, and although top drop is a lesser-known condition, it very much exists and can rear its head when your bondage practice becomes more intense and consuming. Drop can also occur if a scene is ended abruptly, as the short shock of coming out of the moment can leave you feeling somewhat adrift and abandoned.

If you are experiencing sub drop or top drop, you may feel lonely, used, physically detached from the things around you and just not yourself; you may feel antisocial and feel that there's no one you can reach out to. The physical aspects of drop include a low temperature and exhaustion, as well as incoherence—not unlike coming down off drugs, or having a severe hangover.

Aftercare is a huge part of helping people to avoid and recover from drop. As your bondage practice becomes more intense, learn to come back to earth a little more gently; wind down a scene rather than ending it quickly (unless necessary, of course, in which case ending the scene is the priority over everything else), and if your rope bunny is suspended, bring her down softly and slowly. Have a blanket nearby in case your sub becomes cold, and encourage her to lie down for a while until she becomes fully oriented again. The feel of a hard floor can help with this, but then move your sub to a comforting, comfortable place. Bring her water, keep her hydrated and massage her where she aches. Don't forget to extend this aftercare to yourself, or to other riggers who have been playing; all participants benefit from aftercare!

If you find yourself experiencing drop in the days after a scene, ensure that you have the number of a close friend or bondage partner to call; if they can't come to you, you can at least chat with them about how you're

Facing Page: Playing on a couch or other soft surface can avoid issues with diaphragm compression and will keep your sub feeling comfy throughout.

feeling and they can provide you with the support that you need. Keep a self-care kit at home, and include in it some good dark chocolate and things that help you to deal with stress: movies, music, books, photographs—anything that comforts you. You might find that writing materials and art supplies allow you to express your feelings and deal with them, or you might just need to be around someone.

Eating properly can help you to stabilize yourself; although you'll most likely crave carbs, try to eat something balanced; veggies, a little natural fat, whole grains, and foods high in magnesium, zinc and iron will help you to feel better. Simple, low-impact exercise such as walking, swimming or some very chilled yoga can also help to get yourself back to a good place, as can meditation and aromatherapy.

Don't be afraid to ask for emotional support, and try to remember that it will pass; give yourself time and you will get back to a positive, passionate place. Just make sure that next time, your landing is a little softer.

The Connection

Bondage is not an onanistic pursuit. It's not just one person; it's two, or three, or if you've a good amount of stamina, even more. No matter how many people you're playing with, there is a frisson in the air. Tying someone up isn't just a physical thing. It is an intimate connection between partners; an exchange of agency, a visceral exhibition of trust, a letting go. The art and the sex come second to this; the connection is the most important part of any bondage practice.

The connection is the thing that will keep all play partners in a positive mental space when playing. In order for one person to give themselves up entirely, they need to feel great trust in their partner—and that trust needs to be nurtured. Maintaining physical connection is a fantastic way to ensure that your rope bunny feels looked after and considered even when he or she is being swung upside down in a full body harness or trapped in a helpless position and exhibited to others. Just feeling the warmth of your palm on their body will help your bunny to remain in that fluffy headspace that so many submissives love, and will help you to keep a good check on their reactions and circulation. Keep eye contact when

Facing Page: The connection between the rigger and bunny is almost sacred. Eye and body contact should always be maintained.

The connection between play partners (and the photographer!) is the most important thing. Treasure it.

you can; say you partner's name and use soothing words and phrases. They need to feel your presence and your appreciation at all times.

Once at Morpheous' Bondage Extravaganza, I had my bunny suspended and the scene was going well. She was happily swinging and drifting into a floaty space. However, I had had a full hip transplant about nine months earlier (hey, we all get older—it will be your turn too) and didn't have the same level of mobility that I used to have. About twenty minutes into the scene, just after I had got her up and suspended, I caught the toe of my boot on one of the risers on stage and an excruciating pain shot up my leg, right through my hip flexor. The crowd didn't notice; they couldn't see how hard I bit the inside of my cheek to stop from yelling out. However, I had a few friends nearby and I motioned for them to drift into the scene and help me take the bunny down in a sexy and apparently planned way. I had one of my female friends sit under her as we lowered the bunny. The bunny gracefully dropped into my friend's waiting arms where she was petted and stroked in a very loving and erotic way. The crowd was none the wiser. When I felt that bolt in my hip, I knew I couldn't finish what I had planned; the pain in my hip was too great and I needed to pull the plug on it for the safety of both of us. Luckily I had taken precautions, and had friends close by that could help me wrap up the scene in a safe and sexy way, even if it was a little earlier than expected. Never underestimate your friends; they will help you when you need it. The bunny understood that I had been in too much pain to continue the scene safely, and we all finished up feeling satisfied and grateful for each other.

For me, one of the best things about Morpheous' Bondage Extravaganza is the ability to walk around and watch the sparks fly between two people, between the rigger and the bunny. At every event, we have dozens of professionals tying up their bunnies, and the setup of the night means that you can wander around from station to station, watching as the whole thing unfolds. It's truly moving to witness the way each partnership nurtures its connection; some do so by talking to each other in steady tones no matter what is happening, while others prefer to be near silent, their hands and rope doing all the communicating for them. These events exhibit the very unique way that each person likes to experience the connection that they get with their partner when they tie each other up. It's a beautiful thing.

When someone places themselves into your hands, both emotionally and physically, you have a duty to that person. Ensure that you don't let yourself down.

Physical Safety

As an intermediate rigger, you will, by now, have your handy little kit of tools and essentials that stay nearby every time you whip out your rope (or your yarn, or your cord, or in fact anything that you're going to use to bind any part of anyone, even if it's just ribbon). Right? You have your safety shears, your Arnica cream, your carabiners, your suspension ring or whatever it is that you like to bring into your rope play. You have your basic medical training under your belt, your knowledge of your partner's medical history and a phone nearby just in case something goes wrong. You know all this; you've been doing it for a while.

As your style of bondage leaps from beginner to intermediate and the ties become more difficult and more consuming, it can be easy to forget to check in with your rope bunny as often as you should. Don't ever let the process of tying become more important than the safety aspects of bondage. More complex ties and restraints mean more contact points,

and you should always be sure to distribute any stress evenly; if you are tying your bunny in a body harness to suspend her from something, check twice and then once more that the weight distribution will be even and comfortable. Do the fingernail test more often than you think is strictly necessary, especially if you're doing a tie for the first time. It's better to be safe than sorry.

As your skills grow, you'll begin to combine ties and methods to put your own ties together, exploring your creativity. While you do this, it's essential to remember to *never tie a knot on top of a knot*. You need to be able to reach any knot at any given time. If a situation occurs and you need to free your partner, covering one knot with another is very dangerous. As you grow more proficient as a rigger, you should also strive to know more about the body and how it is affected by being in certain positions. For instance, tying your sub's wrists together and up above his head while he is standing can pull the torso taut and make it difficult to breathe as the diaphragm may not be able to work properly. If you tie your sub's hands above his head for too long, the hands will fall asleep. You should know precisely what effect any tie will have on the body before you use it; don't be caught out!

It is not only the rigger that is responsible for bondage safety; all participants in a scene share an equal responsibility to ensure that everyone is safe. Be very aware and present in every moment during a scene; if you are the bunny and you feel light-headed, let your Dom know immediately. If you feel a cramp somewhere in your body, let your Dom know. If you haven't eaten much in the morning and feel your blood sugar start to drop, let your Dom know. You should eat a good, healthy meal a few hours before any bondage scene and make sure that you're well hydrated. That means water, not eight coffees and a tea.

Never practice bondage when you are drunk or otherwise intoxicated. A glass of wine might help to loosen up the body and mind before a play session, but two or three are plain dangerous. If a partner turns up to a scene obviously under the influence, refuse to play and make sure they get home safely. Would you get into a car if someone was drunk behind the wheel? I didn't think so—so why would you let them tie you up and suspend you? The nature of intoxication is that it can make people unreasonable, so if you

Facing Page: Chest ties look fantastic, but be sure to never tie across the neck. It's a risk that's not worth taking.

request to rearrange your session or simply refuse to play with an intoxicated person, they may try to coerce you or say that you're making a big deal of the situation. Don't succumb to this; you are in the right. You aren't being over the top, and they might tell you so, but you have to keep your good reputation and the safety of that person in mind at all times. *There is always going to be another time to play*—but safely, and always sober.

You should never, ever leave a person in bondage. Not ever. If you are playing with a rigger that leaves you bound in any way, for any amount of time, say your safeword, end the scene and never again play with that person. As you leave, let them know why you won't be involved with them again; give them a stern rebuke, for the safety of others. If you are playing with a rope bunny that wishes to be left alone, maybe for the thrill of feeling abandoned, then explain calmly why you won't be able to comply with their request, and after the scene discuss other ways in which you can simulate the feeling of abandonment without putting either of you at risk.

The biggest cause of death in bondage is leaving a person alone when they are bound, so don't take any chances—even with yourself. Self-bondage can be thrilling, but it is simply too dangerous to do it alone. Always have someone in the room with you if you wish to experiment with self-bondage. I also strongly advise against ever having rope tied around the neck. It might look hot in pictures but the risk is not worthwhile; there is simply too much opportunity for something to go fatally wrong. Never place rope or any other material around the neck when practicing

If playing on a hard floor, always check that your sub is comfortable.

Match your outfit to your rope, and you'll feel like a work of art.

bondage. Act like a reasonable and intelligent adult, please. Your health is the most important thing you own. Don't gamble with it in any way.

A final word: Go slow. There is no rush to the finish line here. The focus should be the process. The connection with tying and with your partner is everything. It is the same with dancing, doing yoga or having sex. There are a lot of ways to do it but in the end the rope is just a tool to get you to where you want to be. Listen to your body and to your partner's body. When I teach classes I stress accountability on the part of both the rigger and the bunny. If you're having a great time being tied up by your favorite rigger, you might want to battle through that strange numbness in your fingers so you don't disrupt the scene, but as the bunny it's your responsibility to let the rigger know what is happening to you. It might be that the rope needs to be loosened; it might be that the scene needs to stop. Don't let your eagerness injure you; there is always tomorrow.

Chapter Three

Intermediate Equipment

The chances are that if you've moved beyond the status of an absolute beginner, you've probably already started building up a nice little kit bag of tricks in your bedroom. Who amongst us can resist splashing a little cash on a beautiful bit of rope to sit under our beds or hang on the wall just next to that long oak dining table, ready and waiting to be used at any time of day? Certainly not me, and not you either, I'll bet.

The world of bondage equipment is as extensive as it is alluringly beautiful. From cold, real metal police handcuffs, neckties, leather belts and a whole rainbow of bondage tape to leg spreaders, vacuum beds and even a St. Andrew's cross; you can have it all, and you can find a use for it all too (I do, and I have). But those of us who love rope love it not just because it lets us wind and fold our bunnies into startlingly gorgeous shapes and keep them there, but because of its very nature. Trapping someone in a vacuum bed is an entirely different (but also thoroughly enjoyable) experience from binding a supple, willing submissive into positions that challenge and test her, letting her feel the tug of the material against her skin as she strains and stretches, or watching it encase her as she bends into herself, ready to eventually emerge reborn once again. No; for this, there can be only rope, and for this reason, we will concentrate mainly on rope

Facing Page: The range of different ropes available allows you to flex your artistic creativity as well as your rigging skills!

Some good quality nylon rope in a bright hue is a great place to start.

when discussing equipment.

As a beginner, all you really need is some good nylon rope, some safety shears and some Arnica cream for when your bunny is released and the aftercare begins (you do rub Arnica into the bruises of your bunny, don't you? Of course you do—good girl). However, as we go deeper into more intermediate ties, the need for more specialized equipment arises. You don't want to be using the wrong type of rope for ties that put pressure on parts of your submissive, or be unable to cut through a body harness because you don't have the right things to hand.

As rope bondage becomes a greater part of your life, too, you might find yourself more interested in investing in good quality, handmade equipment that will stand the test of time, and will hold steady through hours and hours of hot, sweaty play—or, perhaps, beautiful rope that will look even more fantastic against the skin of your partner and under the glow of photography lights. Your bondage arsenal will grow as your passion does—

Facing Page: Different rope types and widths will create different marks on the skin of your sub. See what pretty patterns you can make!

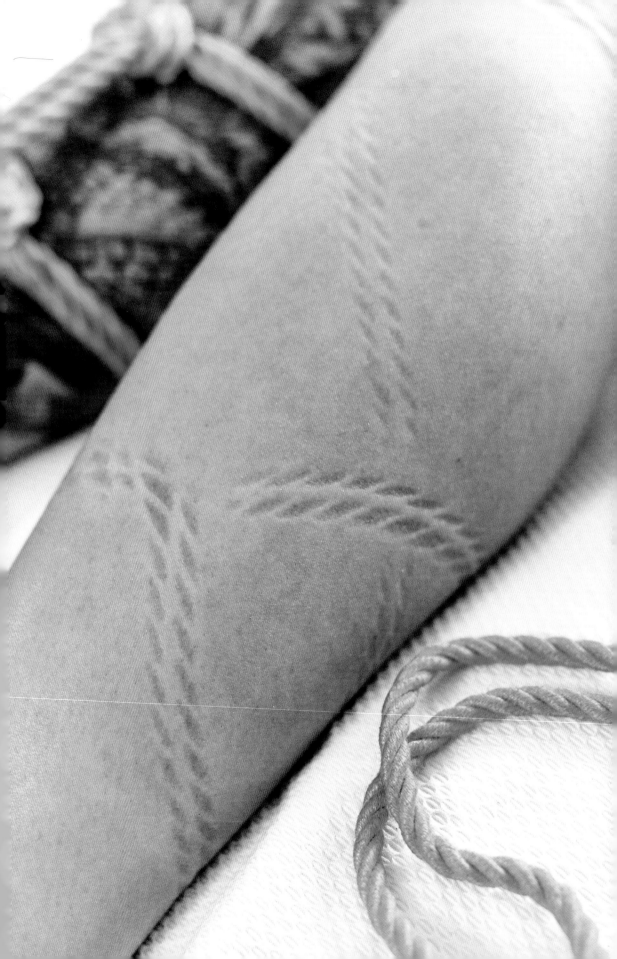

Nylon rope comes in every color under the sun, and some more besides.

which is why my grandma's old chest eventually became too small to hold all my toys and equipment, and why my house now basically looks like a store that specializes in gear for the kinky-minded.

If you can afford it, you should support local and artisan producers of bondage equipment. These people are true artists, and pour hours and hours of work and years of expertise into every piece of equipment that they make. I personally love knowing that the hessian rope pressing into the flesh of my submissive was handwoven by a woman in a cottage not far from my house, and that she can continue on with her art because I supported her. It brings a whole new dimension to the experience!

Different Types of Rope

Although you might already be familiar with nylon rope and the wonderful things you can do with it, there are actually many different rope materials and each one has its own specific pros and cons. Just as types of

paint work better with different styles of painting, these individual ropes suit very different uses. As you move further into your practice, you will want to experiment with these varying materials and see which best lend themselves to your particular style of bondage. Or maybe, like me, you'll be able to find a use for all of them!

There are two distinct categories of bondage rope: Synthetic and natural. As the names suggest, synthetic ropes are made from man-made materials like nylon and paracord, and natural ropes are woven from more hardy, naturally occurring materials like jute, cotton and linen.

Nylon

Nylon is without a doubt the most widely used type of rope for bondage. Not only is it inexpensive, it's also soft, comfortable for your submissive's body and for your hands, and will last forever (or thereabouts). It's flexible and supple, meaning that as you're getting into the zone and your hands are flying, it will do exactly what you need it to do without fighting back. And, as an added bonus, it comes in a whole palette of sumptuous colors, giving your bondage a more artistic twist that will have you reaching for your camera to capture your submissive in his most glorious form. I love binding and tying my submissives in bright nylon as it looks so fantastic in pictures; in fact, think I have every color that they produce—or most of them!

Nylon has a tendency to stretch, which can be good or bad, depending on what you are using it for, but it is also very strong, making it a good choice for suspension ties and harnesses, which benefit from the rope having a little give but still being strong. Nylon doesn't have the same friction level as some natural fiber ropes, making them less "grippy" than things like jute. The main benefit of nylon, however, is that ties will stay solid no matter how much you (or the movements of your sub) tug them around, and will also remain easy to untie, meaning that it is one of the safest types of rope to use. Remember to always keep safety shears nearby regardless of what type of rope you use.

Paracord

Also known by its full name (parachute cord) this is a type of nylon made of multiple strands that are covered by a braided outer layer, which makes it soft and easy to use. The US military and others began using parachute cord instead of natural fiber ropes as paracord didn't break as much and

Uncle Morpheous says you must always keep your rope nice and neat, there's a good little perv.

therefore was a lot more likely to safely deliver paratroops to their location. If your partner is in the military, get her to bring some paracord home and you'll find a million kinky ways to use it!

The term "paracord" is used for different types of thin synthetic rope materials, so be careful to test your own and get to know it before you use it. Much like nylon rope, paracord is supple, soft, durable and hardy, and it also has some stretch too. However, it isn't very good at bearing weight and won't be as strong as thicker nylon rope, so be sure to use nylon rope with a thicker diameter if you're planning on doing suspension ties. Paracord is best used for ties on the arms, genitals and other body parts for artistic ties or decoration, and its low price means that if it gets sticky

(not that I would know how it might get into such a state) or ruined, you can throw it away and won't weep over the cost of replacing it.

Polyester (Dacron)

Polyester rope (also known as Dacron) is also similar to nylon but is more difficult to use due to it being slightly firmer and less flexible. It's also not as strong, so shouldn't be used for weight-bearing ties, and there aren't all that many colors available as the material is difficult to dye. I am not really a fan.

Jute

Jute rope is a firm favorite (no pun intended) with hardcore bondage fans, me included. You might have seen it in the form of Hessian material or burlap; it's a vegetable fiber spun into a coarse, strong, firm thread. It's fantastic at weight bearing, and with a high level of friction it's really great for holding knots.

Jute is the rope most commonly used for shibari in its homeland of Japan, where it's a little easier to source than in North America and Europe. Despite the difficulty of finding real jute rope, the traditionalists among us also love this material as it brings us a little closer to bondage as it used to be: Awkward, uncomfortable, physically demanding and sexy as hell.

I don't care what anyone says. You can never have too much rope.

Cotton

This is the most popular material for natural ropes, given its availability, low cost and ease of use. Some might think that this makes it less interesting, but I disagree; cotton is often twisted or braided, giving you great textures and forms to play with. It's a very simple material to work with, meaning that it can be a great choice for beginners who don't want to invest a lot of money in their new hobby.

The downside to cotton is that it can stretch a lot, especially under tension, and doesn't have a lot of friction. It's liable to slip and stretch, making knots incredibly tight and dangerously difficult to undo. For this reason, cotton rope used for suspension bondage must be of much higher quality (making it much more expensive) with a very high weight-bearing capacity. Unless you're incredibly sure of your rope knowledge, it's best to keep cotton rope for non-suspension ties.

I use a variety of ropes made from different fibers. All the colored rope you'll see in this book is cotton. It's comfortable for the rigger, the bunny and your bank account. As well as being available in many colors, it is easy to dye if you want to do it yourself—which is a whole new way to commit yourself to the practice!

Linen

Linen or flax rope is the smoothest of the natural fibers here, and it is especially soft against supple skin. It's a lot like hemp but without the enticing smell and with a little more of a "fluffy" feel, but for some reason isn't as widely used as jute or hemp. It's very well suited to most types of bondage, and you can even find blends of linen and hemp that have all the strength characteristics of hemp rope with the softness of linen.

Hemp

As a coarse natural fiber, hemp is similar to jute but is heavier, much easier to find in stores and very rough when untreated. Boiling, washing and treating the rope will leave a much smoother rope that's just as good at weight bearing and just as fun to play with. We'll go over treating rope later in this chapter.

Facing Page: More traditional fibers can bring a great sense of history to your rope play—and your role-play!

Our rigger is shocked at how good it feels to use natural fibers. I know the feeling.

Hemp rope has a very particular smell and is a little abrasive on the skin, which is bad news if you need to keep your bedroom activities hidden from your friends, family and employers but good news if you like to walk around showing your rope marks off for all to see. This abrasiveness also makes it a good choice for predicament bondage, in which submissives are placed in uncomfortable or unpleasant contortions. The smell can also work as a little pre-play teaser; some submissives who've had experience with hemp before can be led down the garden path to subspace just by the smell of the rope. It's a beautiful thing to see your partner wriggle and squirm when they smell what you've got in your bag of tricks.

Silk

Now we come to the dangerously expensive portion of the program: Silk. A million worms might have to die to make enough silk rope to bind your bunny, but as he's wrapped in luxurious coils and knots, he'll be glad that they did. If you can't afford to splash out on silk rope, I recommend that

Facing Page: You can dye your own cotton rope if you want even more fantastic colors like this.

Keeping your rope neat and tidy will make playing much easier.

you don't ever touch it, because once you do you'll be seduced by the gorgeous feel of the fibers and you'll be halfway to mortgaging your house to buy miles of the stuff before anyone jumps in and stops you. It's flexible, won't stretch, doesn't cause too much friction and acts in a similar way to cotton, except it feels so much nicer for both you and your rope bunny. Silk does tend to wear out a lot more quickly than more hardy materials like cotton and linen, so if you splash out on some silk, keep it for a treat rather than everyday use; tell your bunny that if he's a good boy, he might get to be tied up in silk at the end of your play session!

Bamboo

It's not just organic babygros and overly expensive kitchen utensils that utilize bamboo; bamboo rope is also relatively popular on the bondage scene, although it remains pricey compared to other options. However, as with silk, if you can afford bamboo you'll find yourself falling very quickly in love with it for its great feel and ease of use. Much like silk, the material is incredibly sexy, very comfortable and will be like putty in your hands—and it will encase your submissive in such opulence that she will never want to escape from your ties. Bamboo has less grip than silk, making it slightly harder to work with, but it is preferable to silk in one major way: It is naturally antibacterial and shines like nylon, making it perfect for sensitive skin and also for bondage photography.

Facing Page: Silk can finish her off nicely. If you know what I mean.

Coconut Coir

This type of rope should be used with caution, and only by riggers who feel they're entirely comfortable with their knowledge of the material. If you're going to experiment with coir rope, which is mercifully inexpensive, ensure that you purchase the highest possible quality, and don't ever attempt any suspensions with it. The material is simply not strong enough to support even the most waiflike of bunnies.

Compared to materials like nylon, coir isn't all that flexible and still poses a challenge in working with it. However, it is more supple than some other, harsher natural fibers and stretches well, meaning that if you want to challenge yourself, this is a good rope to try. It will, however, scratch and nip at your submissive, as the material is harsh and creates friction like it's going out of fashion. If your sub is a bit of a masochist and wants to feel the burn (quite literally) while you play, give coir a go—but stay cautious, ask for feedback often and make sure that your shears would be able to cut through the material at any time. Oh, and buy another tub of Arnica cream; you're going to need it.

What Not to Use

There are a number of other materials used to make rope, including generic polypropylene, manila, sisal and coir. However, none of these are ideal for use in rope bondage, and therefore should be avoided as you go forward. Generic polypropylene is the stiff, scratchy stuff used to make the ropes you'd normally find in hardware stores for cheap. This is both difficult to work with and fairly horrible to skin, so it makes your ties weak and your submissive uncomfortable (and not in the good way).

Manila and sisal, too, are tough and don't knot well, tending to splinter and stick into a submissive's skin. They are widely available and cheap, making them sound like a good idea while you're wandering around Home Depot on a Saturday morning with kinky thoughts in your brain, but trust me: They're no good. Twine is readily available in almost all places, and is cheap and easy to use. However, this should only be used for light finger or toe bondage, and even then, with caution, as it can bite into skin and cut flesh.

Facing Page: Forget the collars and the cuffs—I'm a sucker for a bunny when her makeup matches my rope.

Some natural fibers can cause irritation in some people, so do a test before using any new material on a new submissive. Lightly tie a piece of rope around your sub's wrist for a while, and if no adverse effects present themselves, you're all good to go!

Jute and hemp can be used for suspension bondage as they hold knots well, but sometimes if you tie a knot upside down, it can jam. I haven't needed to cut my ropes but if you do, safety shears are the only thing that will do it safely and efficiently. Fair warning: If you plan on getting jute or hemp ropes wet, the rope will swell and you won't be able to get any of the knots undone. Tie your knots with this in mind and reassess your safety measures before you begin.

Sizes of Rope
Thickness

As we should all know by this stage in our lives, there's no one perfect size—and it's always more about girth than length. This is very true of bondage rope.

Most bondage rope will be between 4mm and 8mm thick, and which you want depends on what you're planning on doing with it. However, for all-purpose rope, you want to go somewhere in the middle; remember Goldilocks. Her perfect first-timer rope bondage purchase would be somewhere around the 6mm mark.

The thinnest rope is around 4mm. This type of rope is best used for non-weight-bearing ties and microbondage, where you tie particular parts of the body and even small areas like fingers and toes. For anything more substantial than this, it will dig too harshly into your rope bunny's skin, and the knots can slip to become far too tight. Remember, you should always be able to untie or free your partner quickly and safely. For these reasons, 4 or 5mm rope is best kept for bondage on a specific part of the body.

On average, most ropes are about 6mm thick. This is a fantastic midpoint between too delicate and slippy and too hard to use. They can bear weight, keep knots where they're meant to be and allow you to rig quickly and smoothly. They can also suspend your submissive without cutting into the skin too badly and will leave gorgeous marks on the body as opposed

Facing Page: A post-play bunny. Covered in rope marks, gorgeously satisfied and totally worn out.

Some types of rope are better for weight-bearing ties than others, and some are better on the soft, fleshy parts of the body.

to searing marks that look terribly painful.

8mm rope will be too thick for most purposes, especially for those starting out. As well as being difficult to tie and to knot with, it's also prone to letting knots slip out. While there are some uses for thick rope, like suspending heavier bunnies, it's best to keep within the 6mm or 7mm range for most uses.

Length

While you'll most likely find yourself buying a number of different lengths of rope as you become more passionate about (okay, obsessed with) your hobby, the Goldilocks rule is a good one to remember here too. Bondage ropes come in many lengths but most fall between 10 feet

Facing Page: Thinner rope can even be woven into hair for a fantastic finished look.

(3 meters) and 50 feet (15 meters), with around 30 feet (9 meters) being the most common.

Shorter lengths of rope can be used for things like microbondage and very simple ties, as well as for performing bondage solely on the arms or the legs. In Japan, ropes of 22 feet (7 meters) are used primarily, so shibari traditionalists often prefer to use these lengths as well. In Japan, new lengths of rope are added as a tie becomes more complex, and the ropes are knotted at the end to make this process easier. However, short ropes can be difficult for beginners, as it can be difficult to judge just what length your tie will require before you start. Keep in mind that the Western body is typically larger than a Japanese rope bondage model so you will need more rope to get the same effect.

While 30 feet is probably the most commonly used length, anything between 25 feet (7.6 meters) and 35 feet (10 meters) is considered average. While this should provide more than enough room to create a relatively elaborate harness tie, it won't leave tons of trailing rope around your feet and getting in your way. As a starter length, this is just about perfect.

However, if you're experimenting with extra-elaborate ties or full-body harnesses, you might find that something a little longer, up to 50 feet, will be better. This will create some difficulty in that there will be a lot of extra rope for much of the tying, but you also won't end up tantalizingly close to being finished only to find that you're half a meter short on a suspension harness. That's no fun at all.

Preparing Your Rope
Treating

Some rope materials, such as jute, linen and hemp (and some other natural fibers), benefit from being treated before use. These types of rope can be washed, and doing so can ease the harshness of the material and make the rope more flexible. Without wanting to sound too romantic about it, it's also really fun to treat your own rope, and if you're anything like me you'll gain something of a new respect for it. Binding your submissive with rope that you've treated yourself brings a whole new dimension to the experience, like eating your dinner from a table that you've made. You can also

Facing Page: For suspensions, consider using a slightly thicker rope. 5mm or 6mm should be good.

eat your dinner off your submissive, if you tie and suspend them correctly.

You'll need to start by cutting your rope down to the desired length. See the section above for help deciding what length that will be. Whip the ends to neated the rope, or simply tie an overhand knot at each end, then coil the rope loosely, securing the coils (loosely again) with string.

Place the coiled rope into a large pan of hot water and bring it to the boil. Place the lid on the pan and keep it on a simmer, checking every now and again to ensure that all the rope is below the water level; as it continues to boil, it might become slightly more turgid and protrude from the water. Cook this way for a couple of hours.

After a few hours, turn off the heat and leave the rope to cool completely. The rope will stay incredibly hot for a long time, so it's best to leave it overnight before you attempt to handle it. If your hands are ruined by hot rope, you can't play, so be careful. In the morning, drain the water from the pan and place the rope into the washing machine on the most delicate cycle there is.

Drying

The easiest way is to dry your washed rope is in a tumble dryer on a medium heat. Clean your lint drawer beforehand, as it is certain to get totally gunked up with rope debris, and don't set the dryer on too high a heat or you'll shorten the rope too much.

After the cycle, the rope will have shrunk a little, so you'll need to stretch and untwist it to get it into prime condition. You can do this by coiling it under your foot and pulling hard, or wrapping it around any secure metal bar or structure. Pull hard several times; you'll feel the stretch come back and some fibers inside break a little. Keep going until all the rope has been stretched back out.

If you don't have a tumble dryer or don't want to use it, you can also just hang and stretch the rope to dry. This should take a day or so, depending on where you live and how warm it is. If you're hang drying, you'll need to stretch the rope before you hang it to dry AND afterwards. Trust me, it's better to put this effort in now than struggle with stiff, short rope for a long time afterwards!

Facing Page: Play with different types of ropes to see which your sub enjoys the most—and which gets her the hottest.

Your kit can be as basic as you want it to be. Some simple rope and some safety shears are all that's really needed.

Oiling

While it's not strictly necessary to oil your rope, it's a relatively easy step and will help you to get that smooth, supple finished product that makes bondage so much fun. There are a number of different oils that you can use, but two common ones are hemp oil and jojoba oil (much like the stuff you'd use to stretch out a piercing).

The next part is easy. Pour a decent amount of the oil onto a cloth and wipe it on in both directions. Now massage the oil in with your hands, taking as long as you care to over it, and leave it a few hours to dry. You can repeat this step if you really want to; it'll improve with every application of oil.

Whipping

No, not that type of whipping; that comes later. What we're talking about here is treating the ends of the rope. No matter what type of rope you buy, you will most likely need to do something to the ends to keep them from fraying and ensure their longevity. This is called "whipping" the ends.

Facing Page: Keep your kit all neat and tidy. Look after your rope and it will look after you.

Some ends will be pre-burned or taped. These are both types of whipping. However, sometimes you will need to whip the ends of your rope yourself, and the best way to do this is by tying and threading.

Basic Bondage Kit

As someone with a little bondage experience until your belt, you should already have a basic bondage kit—but if you don't, here's a great little primer kit to start from. As always, try to buy ethically made equipment and try to consider quality, even if you are on a budget. Never buy substandard equipment that may put someone's health at risk.

> 2 pieces of 30-foot nylon rope, 6mm in diameter
> 1 silk scarf or men's tie
> safety shears
> Arnica cream

For me, this is the bare minimum that any rope bondage aficionado can really get away with. The silk scarf or necktie allows you to easily and quickly bind your bunny's hands or feet without making things too complicated, while the nylon rope is supple and malleable enough for almost all uses, without being too hard on your poor submissive's skin. Nylon rope lasts near forever.

Wrapping your bundled rope in a silk scarf is a beautiful way to store it.

Your bunny will have a strong relationship with the rope she plays with, just as you will.

Expanding Your Kit

If you've had your basics kit for a while and feel that your skill and practice is outgrowing it, it's time to invest in some new equipment.

The first thing to think of is more of the same nylon rope that you've already got. It's not quite as exciting as going out to buy something altogether new, but if you're happy with the quality of your beginner's rope, you might want to think about investing in some different lengths, or slightly different thicknesses.

Let your specific interests guide you in what to invest in next. If you're tending more towards learning about suspension ties, you will want to ensure that your next purchase is some strong, malleable rope; perhaps jute or hemp. If you're tending towards microbondage, why not get some thinner or shorter lengths in cotton or bright nylon? Your local craft store will have oodles of colored yarns and ribbon, which is perfect for microbondage and is so cheap that when you're finished playing, you can just cut it off and throw it away. There are many local artisans that make rope who need your support. All the colored, cotton rope you see in this book was handcrafted by handmaderope.com who have been doing it for almost twenty years. Support your artisans so they can support you.

Chapter Four

Binds for Sex, Binds for Art and My Modern Fusion Style

Believe it or not, not every rigger wants to tie up their submissives for the purposes of ravishing them senseless, and not every rope bunny gets wetter than the rocks at the bottom of Niagara Falls when they're trussed up in coils of rough jute. I know, it's hard to imagine. But it's true.

Historically, rope bondage has been used for a number of purposes. Eastern rope bondage originally began as an offshoot of Hojojutsu, in which practitioners (including Samurai) would restrain their opponents using rope to humiliate them and as a show of power. This practice eventually began to show up in kabuki theatre, Japan's outrageous theatre style, and from there it developed into something of a sexual art known as kinbaku. This style and method became wildly popular through paintings by Seiu Ito, and the new sexual dimension brought a whole new life to Eastern rope bondage.

Over the in West, however, rope bondage existed as an art form first and foremost. Fetish imagery and artwork sprang to popularity in the early days of the 20th Century in the works of John Willie, the founder of Bizarre

Facing Page: Bound subs make great furniture!

Tying the legs can bring about an incredibly intense sensation for your bunny.

Magazine. Alberto Vargas, a Peruvian painter with a kinky streak as long as his arm, also helped to bring rope bondage art to the fore with his beautiful and striking pinup/fetish works. Vargas was probably the most enduring influence on modern fetish art, and his paintings can still be seen everywhere today. However, it was Bettie Page who really catapulted bondage art into the American mainstream when she began to pose for photographer Irving Klaw, who then sold the kinky photos through his mail order business. With her raven hair and playful modeling style, Page was impossible to tear your eyes away from, and she brought about a sense of empowerment for bunnies as well as a brand-new bondage aesthetic. She also looked like she was having the most fun ever.

Of course, the two styles have since influenced each other in myriad ways, not least within my own bondage style, which blends elements of the two. Strangely, it was the advent of the Second World War that brought the very distinct Eastern and Western styles together; the East and West traded many cultural traits during the war, and rope bondage preferences were included in this cross-cultural exchange. War: What is it good for? Rope bondage, apparently.

Shibari

Although the word *shibari* is often used to refer to rope bondage in general, the term is properly used to refer to the artistic practice of rope bondage for aesthetic purposes. However, this definition somewhat sells the practice short; in reality, it's an incredibly moving and intense exchange between partners, with a goal of creating a truly gorgeous piece of physical art. I've heard the practice referred to as "the art of erotic spirituality" before. This should tell you a lot about the practitioners of shibari and how they feel about their rope bondage. For both riggers and bunnies, shibari is a place of spiritual connection as well as intense sensation. In fact, it's been described before as a "method of communication," with the practice of tying being just as important as the final tie. In shibari, rope caresses and responds, and bunnies hum with sexual energy. Riggers seduce and bunnies surrender, and the physical conversation that goes on strengthens the bond between the rigger and their submissive. Many consider it analogous to dance, with the power transferring between the rigger and bunny, and they claim that it achieves as much in presentation as it does in pleasure.

That isn't to say that there's nothing sensual about shibari—far from it. In fact, it's all about sensuality, just as burlesque is all about sex. As well as the sexual energy that exists between the two people, the very practice of tying can help physical reactions take place. By placing knots in alignment with pressure points on the body, riggers can stimulate energy flow and propel their bunny into subspace, that infamous but somewhat difficult-to-find mental place that makes the rest of the world fall away. It's not just the bunny that gets to enjoy this; the rigger, too, can reach a sort of meditation, in which they're filled with sensuality.

Interestingly, shibari actually allows for a flipping of the traditional power dynamic of bondage. While most think that the rigger has all the power when it comes to tying, many shibari bunnies in fact feel powerful and pampered in their rope, as they become the masterpiece, the artwork, the living statue.

Shibari can also form a part of foreplay, getting you both warmed up before the main event. As well as easing you both into an intense headspace that allows for fantastic sex, bondage can be a way to tease and tantalize your partner. Being trussed up and even suspended can get you going but if your rigger won't touch you, it can be teasing in a way that will make you desperate for more. A purely nonsexual bondage session can be the sexiest thing there is. Your bunny will be begging for a little play afterwards. Whether or not you keep her hanging (metaphorically, of course) is up to you!

Shibari tying tends to be intricate and quite beautiful; the final look of a tie is as important as the sensation for the submissive. Shibari riggers use a number of shorter ropes (as opposed to the longer ropes of kinbaku) so that harnesses and more difficult ties can be done in stages and removed in different pieces too. This allows for decorative and practical knots that are as attractive as they are useful.

Kinbaku

As a term, kinbaku refers to rope bondage for sexual and artistic purposes, as distinct from shibari, which is bondage solely for art.

When it comes to tying for sex, your primary considerations are threefold: Safety, positioning and finally aesthetics. Safety should be at the forefront of your mind always, but when you're hoisting a leg up and pointing a bottom in the air to get the best position to enter your submissive, you shouldn't let safety be your second thought. Even when you're spreading his cheeks wide open and making sure his cock hangs low for a cheeky reach-around while you peg him, you should be making sure that no knots are digging into him or bearing his weight, no rope has slipped to around his neck (EVER), and always, always that his circulation is strong (he won't be able to keep that erection if it's not).

Positioning is key when it comes to ties for penetration. The sub won't be able to move, so it's up to the rigger to ensure that everything's comfortable and accessible. There's nothing worse than spending half an hour binding your partner into the most delicious body harness and folding

Facing Page: Consider using a pillow or something soft to support your bunny's back when playing on a hard floor.

her this way and that only to find that you need to crouch slightly for optimal thrusting and you have to stop because it gives you that shooting pain up your left calf. No one is satisfied in that situation, and you'll have a hell of a time explaining to your physiotherapist why your hamstring is tighter than a duck's butt.

You also shouldn't try too hard to emulate what you might have seen in porn, in fetish photography or even in bondage exhibitions; the reality of those situations is very different from the reality of your bedroom or dungeon. Whilst fetish porn might show a submissive facedown on a thick wooden chest, her ankles and wrists high in the air behind her head, her pigtails wound around thick jute and tied to her feet, the truth is that such a position can be incredibly dangerous if the diaphragm doesn't have room to move against the wood, and combined with the overextension of the head and feet, things can get unsafe really quickly. Of course, on set, there are many people checking that all performers are safe and well, and though it might seem that the submissive is pounded senseless for ten minutes at a time, she isn't. Shots are stopped for more lube to be applied, for the performers to get hard again and for lighting to be adjusted. It's not real, it's make-believe, so don't try to do exactly what you see onscreen. It can be underwhelming at best and dangerous at worst.

Real-life bondage for sex can be—no, *is*—much sexier than the hardcore stuff you see online. While we all like the idea of getting all of our orifices stuffed by strangers while we're tied by the hands and feet and unable to resist (wait, you don't?), a real-life bondage situation when all participants feel safe and cared for underneath all the power and danger play is so much more intense that it's basically apples and oranges. Don't judge your own sex life, or your own bondage practice, by what you've seen in porn. It's better than that. Porn is entertainment, nothing more and nothing less. You wouldn't learn how to parachute from a Hollywood movie, so don't try to learn how to tie someone from porn. Learn bondage from this book, from the experts in the field. A film set is only a film set.

You should also bear in mind that ties for full mobility restriction and ties that facilitate good sex are hardly ever the same thing. While your favorite bondage porn site might show a cute blonde getting pounded while

Facing Page: Chest and upper arm ties can be incredibly intricate and just as gorgeous.

74

If your sub has been bad, tie her before a spanking. She'll soon learn her lesson.

she's pinned down to a table and unable to move even a finger, the reality is that that's not an optimum position for either of you to enjoy yourselves. You want to be able to reach all the good bits of your partner and get all your good bits inside of your partner rather than only getting halfway in and leaving her frustrated because you've tied her in the wrong way. Before you start tying your partner, think about your favorite positions and how bondage can help you to enhance those positions. When it comes to tying for sex, the rope should be there as a facilitator, not as something to work against. Whether it's simply tying your partner's wrists to the bed frame while you take him from behind, or suspending him in a full body harness to spread his buttcheeks and get full penetration, make it work with what you already like.

When it comes to bondage for sex, I am a big fan of anything that puts the other person in some sort of doggie-style position. They can be lying on their sides or on their knees with their face in the sheets but they should be comfortable enough. Even a position you will see later in the book, with the hands crossed across the front to each opposing hip, is a great one once you get them on the bed.

Of course, we're not just limited to rope here. If you prefer something a little kinder on the skin, there's bondage tape (made for purpose, with no adhesive on either side), plastic wrap and a whole host of other materials. By binding someone with plastic, you can give their skin a nicer experience (if they don't like the feel of rope, that is) and you can rip the plastic wrap to get at their fun parts whenever you feel like it! Bondage tape has the benefit of being very easily undone and being completely nonthreatening to newbies, plus you can reuse it—so if you free someone's wrists you can tie their feet with the same piece of tape! This is useful if you're tying for sex and want to flip between positions quickly (and who doesn't?). However, with bondage tape you'll need to be careful of circulation, and with plastic wrap you'll need to be constantly aware of your partner's body temperature, as they can heat up quickly. Just keep placing a finger to their skin; no need to make it a big deal, unless you want to play Doctor and Patient, in which case lube up your rectal thermometer and go wild!

A Little of Column A, a Little of Column B

We live in exciting and interesting times. Cross-cultural appreciation for both the origins of the Japanese style and the melding of the Western style has brought about a fusion style that is exciting and challenging. This cross-cultural aesthetic isn't anything new. In fact there are cyanotypes by Francois Jeandel in the Musée d'Orsay collection from the 19th Century that clearly capture rope bondage; the scenes shown are so similar to contemporary ties that they could have been shot yesterday, right down to the metal ring you will see in so many online shibari photos of today. As I've said a hundred million times, there is nothing new under the sun, only how we do it!

One will find very strict and disciplined ways of doing certain patterns in shibari. Traditionally, one has had to practice the shibari style for years before branching out and developing a unique style. What I have found with rope bondage in America is that the same rigid system in place for learning has been opened up to personal interpretation much more over the past five years. My good friend Midori wrote a definitive book on rope bondage in 2001 and that really was the first time an English audience could appreciate and understand the terminology, the approach and the patterns to rope bondage with a Japanese foundation. Midori's book appreciated the erotic struggle, the squirm and twist of the body while bound. It was a seminal

Mastering rope makes you 100 percent more sexy. Guaranteed.

book and helped kick off the shibari movement in North America. At the same time another friend of mine, Lew Rubens, was working in the style and inspiration of the Western Bondage greats such as John Willie where tight, restrictive ties focused on immovable restraint. A different approach and a different aesthetic but with the same end goal in mind: The consensual erotic restraint of one's partner. These two styles have since come together in contemporary bondage of the style that is shown in this book.

At my annual all-night rope bondage event, Morpheous' Bondage Extravaganza, we showcase the best contemporary rope bondage for a solid twelve hours. We beam this bondage adventure across the web, and we're proud to show the whole spectrum of bondage styles—from shibari to kinbaku, from modern to classic—and you're just as likely to see giggles and hysterical laughter as you are to see two people engaged in an intensely sexual performance. We're thrilled to be able to show the whole world how beautiful and creative rope bondage can be.

A little side note here: One of the subtle variations I have noticed with rope bondage techniques in Asia compared to in Europe or North America is that if you are an American, for example, your knots and wraps will appear to be backwards to the Japanese style. I believe this is simply because in the West, we process information left to right, whereas in Japan magazines and books are read the opposite way. Translated to the practice of bondage, this means that an American would tie left over right, whereas a Japanese rigger will do it right over left. It is an interesting observation and if you are studying knot work from a different part of the world, be aware of this. It may explain why you find yourself lost in a particular tie: Maybe it isn't the tie, maybe it is just the way you're looking at it!

But back to the fusion. As the Asian and European/American styles have melded together, bondage has become as much about sex as it is about aesthetics. Tying for sex and tying for aesthetic expression aren't mutually exclusive activities. Personally, I like all my art to be totally fuckable, which is why I'm no longer welcome at the New York Guggenheim. For me, bringing together elements of shibari and kinbaku creates the sexiest and most beautiful type of bondage, one that is a process of pleasure from beginning to end, and one that's as much about creative expression as it is about sexual fulfillment. It can be a way to enhance or challenge the usual power play dynamics in your relationship. For instance, you might be in a normally D/s relationship, but when it comes to rope bondage, the submissive might be the rigger and the Domme the willing subject. If, like me, your camera is never too far away from you, trussing up your partner can be a sexually charged creative endeavor to get you both hot and desperate, when you put the camera away and take advantage of his vulnerability. You can use intricate and difficult knots to slowly caress your partner into a full body harness, spreading her wide open however you want her.

The ties in this book can be used however you want them to be. It's possible to approach bondage with different perspectives on different days; we're not always hypersexual beings after all (not even me!). You can use the ties in this book as a way to connect with your partner in a way that is beyond sexual; to honor their bodies, their emotions, their willingness to be putty in your hands.

Or you can just fuck them silly. Whichever floats your boats.

Chapter Five

Easy Intermediate Ties

All right; enough chatter. Let's get to the good stuff: The ties.

The ties in this chapter will utilize some of the knots and ties you should already know from my previous books. These are all relatively simple ties, but are still beyond what would be considered basic. They will also form the building blocks for some of the more intricate designs in other chapters, so make sure that you have mastered these before you move on!

The ties in this chapter and the subsequent chapters all appear in order of difficulty, from easy to more challenging. For this reason, I recommend working through them in the order they've been shown.

As you'll see in the next few chapters, I use a variety of rope made from different fibers. All the colored rope shown in these photos is cotton. I like to use cotton because it is soft, durable and won't break the bank. It also takes dye better than other rope fibers, so you can have a rainbow of colors if you want to put in the work to dye the rope yourself.

Facing Page: Rope and role-play go hand in sexy hand.

Simple Chest Harness

This is a terrifically easy tie to get you into creating a chest harness for your partner.

1 Start by taking the middle of the rope, fold it over so you have the middle and wind it around the chest, under the arms, twice. 2 When you come back to the center, cross the lines, one up, one down. 3 Here is a close-up so you can better understand. 4 Samantha is sticking her finger under the wraps so she can create space to pull the rope through. Do the same. 5 Now she just makes a simple knot.

6 And tighten it down. Now you will have a non-constrictive set of bands that wrap around the chest, above the breasts and ready for the next step. **7** Make another two turns around the body, but this time under the breasts. **8** It should be below the breasts, but still on the rib cage. **9** Repeat the exact same hitch you did for the first set of wraps by tucking it under.

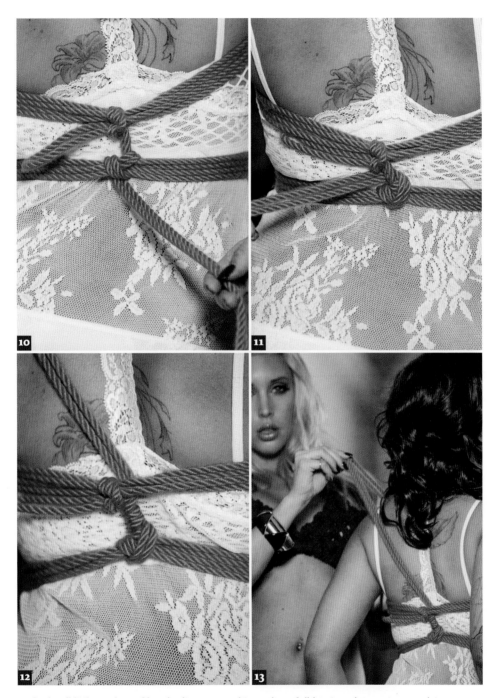

10 And pull it through. **11** You don't even need to make a full knot, as long as you make a minimum of three twists or turns of the rope around the vertical stem of the rope and around the wraps. **12** To make it look pretty, Samantha is winding some of the extra rope around the vertical stem. **13** Come up and over the shoulder.

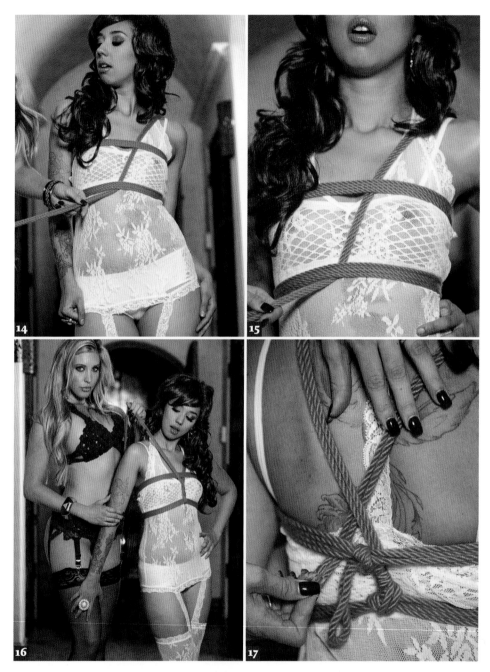

14 Now you are at the front. Notice how the chest wraps are nice and flat with no twists? This makes it more comfortable. Bring the rope down and under the bottom set of wraps. **15** Here is a close-up. **16** To make it fancy, wrap around the line that came down to the bottom a few turns before coming up and over the other shoulder. **17** At the back, tuck it under the first set of wraps and tie it off.

18 If you have another length of rope, you can make a leash for your cute partner!

Sweetheart Chest Tie

The sweetheart chest tie incorporates the basics of weaving into the double chest wraps for a beautiful variation of a typical chest tie. The beauty in it is that during play, your rope bunny doesn't have to have their hands tied and they still get to be tied and feel beautiful, making this a great choice for bunnies relatively new to bondage.

1 Here we have Mosh tying up Ana with some gorgeous orange cotton rope. Stand behind your partner and put the first wrap one above the breast and the other below it so you have it on a diagonal. 2 Here is what the back looks like, see how it is crossing the body diagonally? 3 Come through the loop in the back and go back the other way in the same direction so you will have a total of four bands crossing the chest, diagonally. 4 Starting in the back, change the bias of the diagonal, so you start to build the weave at the crossing point right between the breasts. Every time you come to the rope already laid, you should go over/under in alternating steps. 5 Exactly like this.

6 Come around the back and then to the front and weave the next line over/under to the opposite of the one you just did. **7** Now will be a good time to add rope to the lines you are using. Tip: That can be found in my previous book *Bondage Basics* or the simple and sexy HOTO tie in this book. **8** Now that it is pretty, let's make it secure. From the back come up over the shoulder and weave down over/under the wraps. **9** Come under the wrap and then back up and over the shoulder and weave it into the back wraps. If you've kept all the lines smooth and twist free, this will be a very comfortable tie for them to lie down on the bed without a large knot in their back.

10 We don't even need to make a knot in the back, just weave under the center and then travel back up over the opposite shoulder. **11** And like the other side, drop it down vertically and weave over/under. **12** Here is the only tricky part. Now that the weaving is done you will sneak the rope between their arm and body and go over the bottom wrap. **13** It should look exactly like this.

14 Here is a close-up of how the lines should be running as you head towards the back again, between the arm and the body. **15** Do the same for the other side. **16** Both sides should be symmetrical. **17** Don't forget the one or two finger rule: Even if it is snug, you should always be able to slip a finger or two under the rope if it is the right tension.

18 To cap off this tie, Mosh wanted to add a few wraps around Ana's gorgeous legs so even though her hands are free, she still feels restricted.

Modified Prayer Chest and Arm Tie

This tie is a great way to take your skills from novice to awesome. It has a few more wraps and turns but is very effective as bondage, especially if you have a partner who isn't flexible enough to put their arms behind their back.

1 Start with a simple double cuff or double-column tie that is covered in my last book. **2** Have them bend at the elbows and bring their hands to their chest. Wrap the rope around their torso, twice. **3** Come back over the line that runs to their wrists. Pass under it. **4** And pull the initial rope back towards their other shoulder like this. It will help pull the rope back to vertical and make the next steps look cleaner. **5** Make a few winds around the area where the rope crosses. It isn't important that this is a "real" knot, just a few winds are fine as long as you keep tension on the rope.

6 Now pull the rope up and over the shoulder and pass it through the armpit like this. **7** Pass it over the wraps around the torso and back through under the arm. TIP: Make sure the wraps are on the arm, below the shoulder enough that they don't want to slip up and off. **8** Now follow the line back you just made so you have a four line strap coming over the shoulder and pass it under the initial line that started at the wrists. **9** Make one wrap under and around so we can change direction and head over the other shoulder. **10** Once you travel over the shoulder you should now make another cinch like you did before and then trace that line back to the point of origin, right in the center of the chest. **11** And drop down in the space between the wrists and the chest.

12 Looking great! Seth has her all ensnared.

13 Now bring the rope out front in between the arms. **14** Now we are going to do a double column tie around the bent arm. Keep the tension on the rope and wind it twice around the arm, about four inches up from the inner elbow. **15** You will now be doing a cinch on the wraps. **16** Bring the rope up from underneath and pass it over the ropes and then back down. **17** It will come out to the back. Move across the back and do the same on the other arm.

18 All yours to play with now! This tie is a great one for when you want to lay someone on their back and play with them.

Gun Tie

This tie is one of my all-time favorite "go-to" ties. It is easy but looks difficult, and it gives your rope bunny more movement in their neck than if their wrists were clasped behind the head.

1 Start with a simple one-column tie around the wrist. 2 It should look just like this, with enough room between the wrist and rope cuff. Don't worry; it won't slip off before we are done.

3 Ask them to gently move their arm up behind their back. 4 This is the first part of this tie.

5 You will need them to bend their arm just a little higher for this tie. **6** You are going to do a two-column tie around the bent arm. **7** Remember the wraps from the Modified Prayer tie? The same principal applies. Wrap around the arm. **8** And then cinch between the two parts of the arm, just like this.

9 Now get them to fold their other arm back towards the spine and start wrapping it. TIP: If this is an uncomfortable tie, the "bad" uncomfortable, don't do it. Some people can bend this way and others cannot. **10** You don't need to do the wrap in between the arm, this upper arm can just have the cinch knot stop right in the middle between the arms. **11** Cinch it tight. **12** Now bring the rope down towards the first arm.

13 The rope should be a comfortable level of tightness. Check in with your rope bunny. **14** And pass it through the cuff of the first hand. **15** After it passes through the cuff, you are going to cinch it off so it can't move. **16** Here is a close-up of where you should be right now. **17** After it is cinched, you can use up any excess rope by winding it around the two lines you just created so it looks neat and tidy.

18 Here's how it will appear from the front! Totally gorgeous and utterly sexy.

Variation of a Leg Binder Tie

This is a very easy tie for binding the legs all the way down. It follows a repeating pattern. Take your time and keep it fun. Tip: If you have thinner legs, a small cloth object like a tea towel between the knees will make it more comfortable.

1 Start with one wrap around the body, below the hips, where the body narrows up on the thighs, pulling the end through the loop. **2** Wrap around the legs a second time, pull the end through the loop you just made at the back. **3** Now come between the legs and over the four bands at the front. Keeping some tension on the rope will ensure this all stays nice and neat and won't fall apart on her legs.

4 Here is a longer shot. Notice that the wraps are nice and even around Ana's thighs and the rope that came through the center and over, goes back between her legs whence it came. **5** When you come back through, make a wrap around all the bands. **6** Now, come down to a spot right above the knees, around the legs and behind the vertical line. Again, keep some tension on the rope and everything will stay put while you are tying. **7** Come around a second time, so you have a matching four bands in the front as the thigh tie. Pull your rope through. **8** See, it is all starting to take shape! Come from the back to the front, between the legs and over the bands like this.

9 Return to the back and give it a snug tug. You should be running out of rope at this point.

10 Take the last of the length and wrap it around the back, up the vertical rope, in a decorative manner, tie it off and tuck in your ends. **11** Start with a new length of rope. Repeat the first steps, this time just below the knees. **12** Wrap it around twice. **13** And like before, knot it in the back.

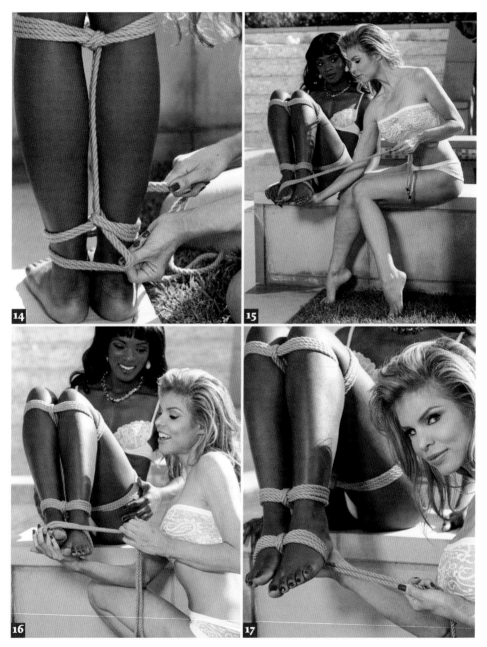

14 Dropping it down just above the ankles, continue the pattern with two wraps making four bands. **15** When you get to the back, again, make a knot and bring it over the front and return to the back, between the legs. **16** You can stop here but if you are a foot enthusiast, come from the back and begin to wrap the feet, right across the arches of the feet. **17** Pull the rope up between and return to the back. Only this time find a place to knot it up on the vertical rope above the ankles in the back so the knot isn't rubbing in between the feet.

18 And don't forget to show your rope bunny some love.

Classic Spread Eagle with a Rope Slipper

This is a more elegant variation of the classic spread eagle tie. You will weave a lovely rope slipper for the feet that will be far more beautiful and comfortable than a simple single-column tie. Like other ties in the book, it uses a repeating pattern and the weave you build will help you with the more sexy and complicated ties, like the Leg Weave, later in this book!

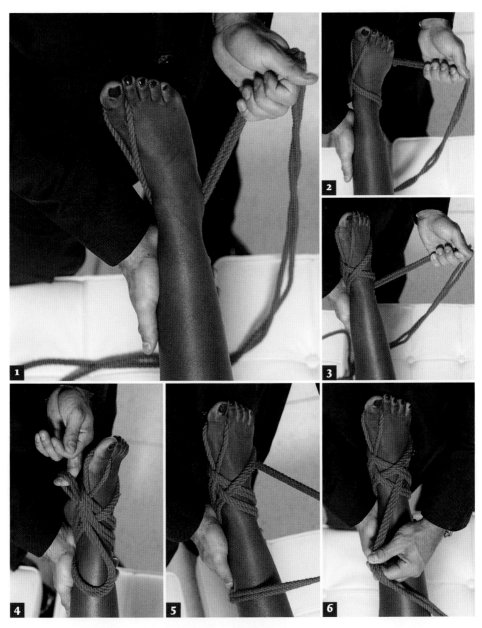

1 Here we have Ana's gorgeous foot in Johnny's hands. He has taken the middle of the rope and placed the loop over the big toe and around the back of the foot, up above the heel. 2 Now he brings the rope up over top of the foot, crosses and heads towards the back. 3 Follow the rope you just did, laying it beside the rope and come again up over the ankle. Be careful not to twist or cross your lines. 4 Alternate your lines, over/under as you get to them. This foundation of the weave will keep the entire tie secure as you build it. 5 See how pretty it is looking? 6 Come around the back, and over/under the existing wraps.

7 The beautiful thing about this tie is you can tie each hand and foot separately as you fool around before securing them tight.

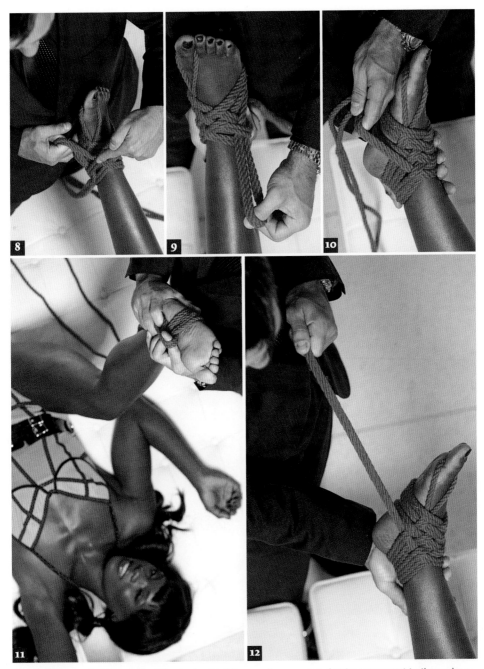

8 Almost finished! Wrap around the foot a third time and weave over/under as you get to the various lines. **9** Tip: It is easier to pull the rope through when it is close to the foot rather than trying to feed it in, free end first. **10** You should have a nice rope slipper built up now. **11** Here is a what the bottom of the foot should look like. Notice how they are just flat wraps, no knots or twists. **12** One last wrap, heading to the bottom.

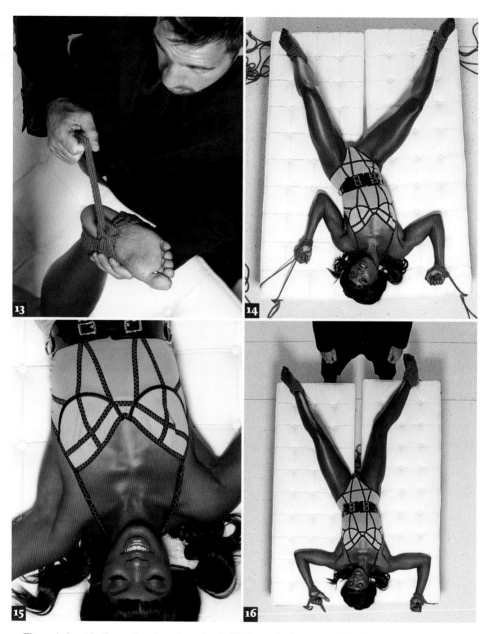

13 The only knot in the entire piece is a simple hitch on the bottom of the foot where the tension will secure it to the furniture. This will keep the foot nice and comfortable as it pulls evenly all across the tie. **14** Once the hitch is finished, you are ready to tie your partner to the bed or chair or chaise…be creative! **15** Keep the mood fun and light. Laugh and giggle and tickle a bit. We call this "play" for a reason. **16** You can do the exact same tie to the hands, just start with the thumb as you did with the big toe, wrap around the back of the hand and alternate over/under the wraps for a very comfortable tie.

17 When you get them all tied down, you can either tuck all the loose ends under the furniture or leave them loose like this for more visual interest. Enjoy!

Simple and Sexy HOTO Harness with Hands in Front

This tie is perfect for partners who have a hard time folding their hands all the way behind their back.

1 Begin by wrapping the folded rope around the body and pulling the free end through the loop.
2 Here is a close-up for you. **3** Cinch it off and run the free end up and over the shoulder, making sure there are no twists in the rope. It should lay flat against the body for comfort. **4** You will cross diagonally between the breasts, wrap to the back, cross over the knot and then cross the chest in the opposing direction. **5** Just like this.

119

6 The back should look exactly like this. **7** Have your partner hold her hands in front of her and wrap once around the lower part of the upper arm. **8** Then wrap around once more. **9** Tip: When you run out of rope, here is how you attach more in a simple but effective way. Always have one longer than the other. I like ropes with knots (or buttons as we call them) on the ends. Fold the longer one back on itself so the loop is the exact same length as the short one.

10 Taking the new rope, make a Lark's Head knot and place it over the end and behind the knot. The loop will add enough mass and friction that it won't slip off if you keep the rope snug.

11 Let's continue! Now make another set of wraps around the upper part of the upper arms, all the way around, twice. **12** Whenever you want to finish off a wrap, tuck it under so it is closer to the skin, rather than over the rope. It will look neater. You are going to head up and over a shoulder again. **13** Cross over the shoulder to the front and down to the bottom wrap, tucking it through and then head up.

14 Then cross behind your original crossing lines and back down. **15** And back up just like this. You want both sides to be symmetrical, so it takes a little practice. **16** I like to mix up my bondage with silk or nylon scarves. They are almost as strong as rope and add visual interest. **17** Tie a handy scarf around the wrists.

18 And she is all yours to play with!

Modified Ebi Tie for Western Bodies

This is a modification of a classic "Shrimp" or "Ebi" tie, named because the person is folded forward at the waist. Western bodies don't bend as well as professional bondage models you may have seen elsewhere, so I have come up with a great compromise for rope bunnies that like the cross-legged position. This tie allows for that position but puts much less stress on the upper back and chest. This is about making it "real."

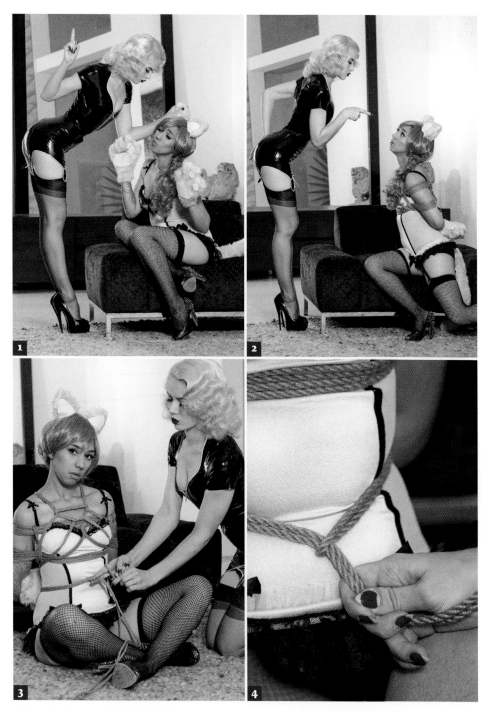

1 First: Catch a cute kitty girl. **2** Then, get them to just suddenly "appear" in a chest tie. Hollywood magic at work! **3** Get her to sit cross-legged as Mosh is making Kerry do here, while she brings a loop around her waist. **4** A simple Lark's Head knot is a great starting point.

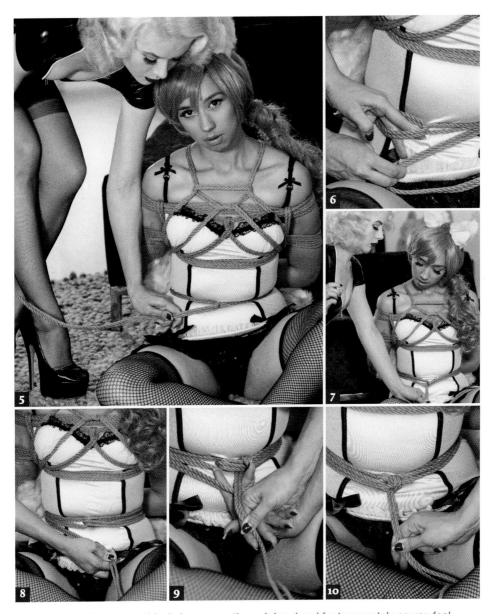

5 The beautiful thing about this tie is you can tie each hand and foot separately as you fool around before securing them tight. **6** Start with a simple double cuff or double-column tie that is covered in my last book. **7** Have them bend at the elbows and bring their hands to their chest. Wrap the rope around their torso, twice. **8** Come back over the line that runs to their wrists, pass under it. **9** And pull the initial rope back towards their other shoulder like this. It will help pull the rope back to vertical and make the next steps look cleaner. **10** Make a few winds around the area where the rope crosses. It isn't important that this is a "real" knot, just a few winds are fine as long as you keep tension on the rope.

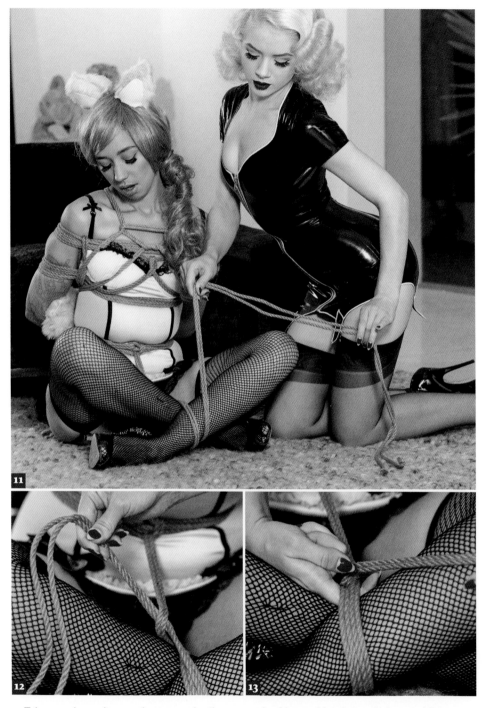

11 Take your long piece and come under the crossed ankles and begin to wind around them.

12 After two wraps, cross the line behind the line that came from the waist. **13** Stick your finger under and through the wraps around the ankles and cross the line over them.

14 And then under. **15** It should look like this. Doing it this way ensures you create a non-constrictive tie around the ankles, so the tension will be on the line to the body, and not squeezing the ankles in a bad way. **16** Come back under the original waist band like this, keeping the right amount of tension on the line. You want it to be nice and even. **17** I like to finish off by wrapping extra rope around the support line you just made. It keeps it looking neat and clean.

18 Now your rope kitty is ready to be all sexy for you.

Chapter Six

Medium Intermediate Ties

In this chapter, we'll start putting together some different building blocks to create composite ties, and we'll also look at more intermediate versions of ties you might already know.

As your bondage becomes more intricate, and the ties more difficult, it's incredibly important to go slow, and, as ever, to keep safety at the forefront of your mind. In this chapter and the next, you'll see layers of rope, compression of body parts and ties that go around bits of your sub that you may not have used before. For this reason, take extra care that what you're doing is safe and comfortable. Practice makes permanent, and if you do these ties incorrectly or unsafely the first time, you're likely to keep doing them that way forever. Go slow, check back to the photo essays time and time again, and always check in with your bunny. Remember: It's a journey. Enjoy it!

Facing Page: It's not just subs that love to be tied.

Chest Tie for Men

When you tie a woman's chest, the breasts help stop the rope from shifting and sliding. Men, however, typically have more prominent pectoral muscles and less fat on their chest, so for a men's chest tie, the same steps are taken but you just pull a little harder to keep the rope situated tight.

1 Start with a simple spread cuff tie. You want the wrists to be apart for comfort with this.

2 Like this. You have done this before I am sure. The magic happens with the rest of the tie.

3 After the wrists are tied, pass the rope around the body. **4** And then back through the cuff of the opposite wrist. Pull the free end back towards his back.

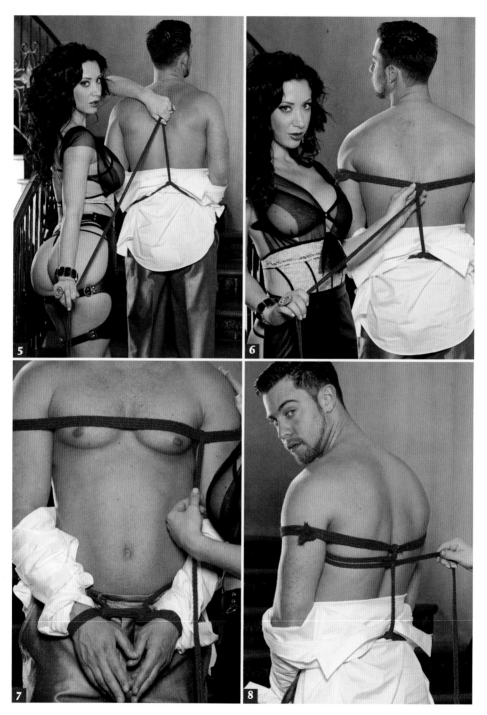

5 Come to the back and then pull the line vertical. **6** Two wraps around the body, over the arms. The rope should be around nipple height. **7** Pass the free end under the arm and over the wraps in the front. **8** Then pull it back to the center and cinch it to the middle rope.

9 Do exactly the same thing to the other side. **10** Now it gets even hotter! Jayden takes the rope and will make another second set of wraps around Seth's arms. **11** All the way around the body trapping the arms under the wraps. **12** Do the same cinch ties between the body and the arms as you just did.

13 Then return to the back where everything started. Make a cinch. **14** Now you are going to change direction. Go up over the shoulder, down the chest to the bottom wraps, pass the rope under them and bring it back over the shoulder to the back. This creates a beautiful separation between the pectoral muscles and really makes them stand out if it is the right tightness.

15 Finish with a cinch in the back. **16** You can make it a simple cinch or even a bow. Because his hands are tied in front he won't be able to reach back to untie himself.

17 This is a great tie for you to make your man helpless. It also works well by laying him down on the bed so you can ravish him. Since his hands are secure in the front he won't be lying on them uncomfortably.

Chest Tie with Crossover

This chest and hand tie forms a strong foundation upon which to build more complicated ties. It is classic and elegant. Here Kerry ties Blair with classic jute rope that is very traditionally used in the Eastern style.

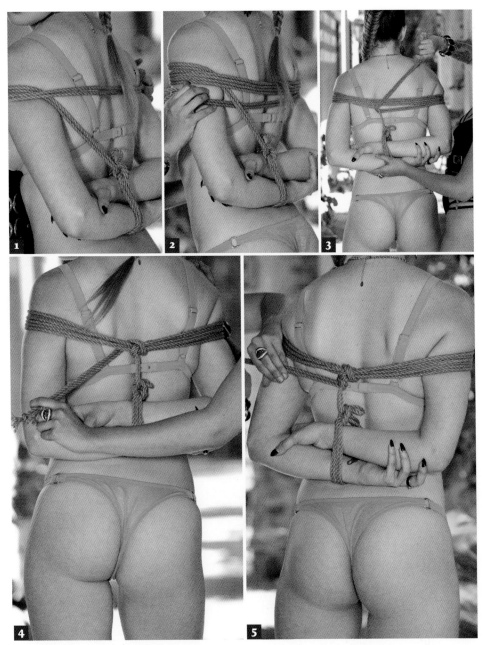

1 This tie begins with a single-column, non-constrictive tie around the wrists. Then the free end of the rope is wound around, over the outside of the arms. 2 Wrap around the arms three times. 3 The last time it winds around the shoulders, it tucks under the vertical rope and then changes direction back towards the right side so the vertical rope is straight up and down. 4 Run the rope up, over and back just like this. 5 The rope is then wrapped over the change of direction so that it locks into place. Like this.

6 Come around to the front, lower and under the breast and at the midpoint bring the rope up, tuck it over the very top rope and then come back down and follow the line under the breast as you bring the rope around to the back. **7** Run the rope underneath the vertical line you have created. **8** Once you come around the back, continue around the body until you have two more full wraps of the body and knot it like this at the back. **9** The rope used for cinching should cross over both sets of wraps, instead of like others in the book that only have it crossing one set of wraps.

10 Tip: Gently pull the rope through. It's easy to pinch the tender part of the underarm. Go gently. **11** Bring it out through the back, wrap it up and around the vertical line and under the rope wraps so it exits underneath when it gets to the top.

12 Bring the free end up between the body and the arm and make a cinch on both sides. Return to the back. Then bring the rope from the back and come up underneath the side and over the shoulder. Tuck it under the back knot and then come back over so that there's a vertical rope, symmetrical on both sides, that travels up and over the shoulders.

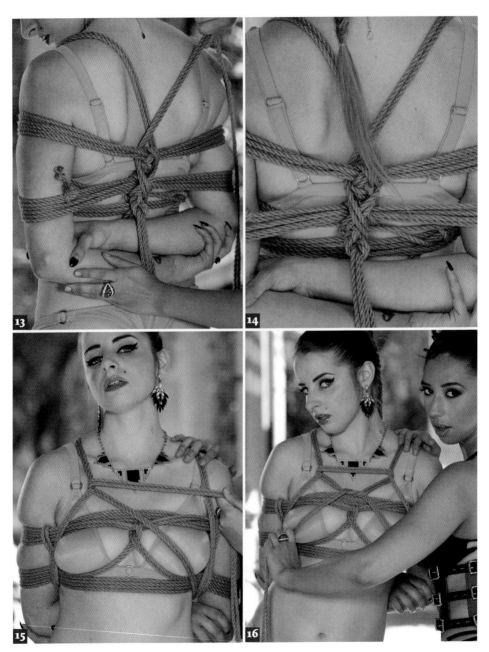

13 Come over the wraps, back up under, keeping all the lines nice and neat and straight and upwards. **14** The back should look nice and neat like this. **15** Come back up under the lower cinch and cross the breasts to the opposing rope that travels over the shoulder, make a turn under it and then move to the other shoulder rope. **16** Here is where the artistic flair comes into play. As you cross back towards the opposing side, make a quick turn in the rope right on the breastplate. Then bring it under the other arm and around to the back. Knot it off neatly.

17 It should look just like this! Neatness counts: Make sure the wraps aren't crossed over, and as with any bondage, if the rope is too tight, loosen it so that it is comfortable. Your partner can always let you know if everything feels okay.

Chest Tie with Legs

This tie is a way to secure the legs that uses a diamond pattern traveling from the knees up to the chest harness, binding the legs all the way up. It is pretty and easy to build once you get the pattern straight.

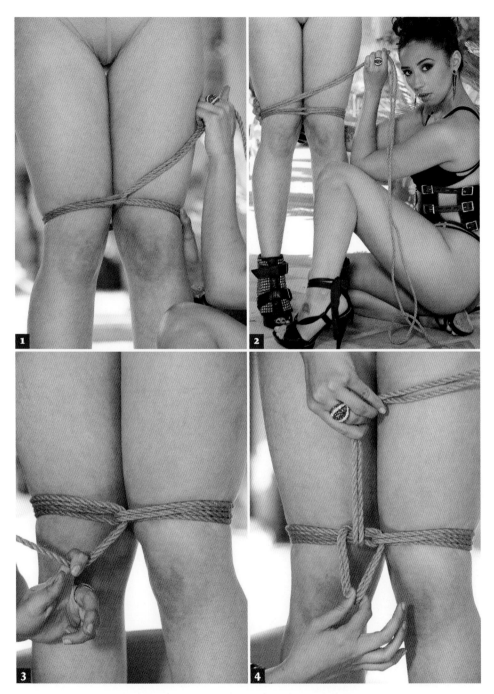

1 Start with a loop around the legs, just above the knees, and pull the end through. **2** Then wrap around the legs and come back to your starting point. **3** Pull it through the original loop or Lark's Head knot which we have seen many times before in this book. **4** Secure it with a hitch. Here is a macro view of how the hitch works just before you pull it tight.

145

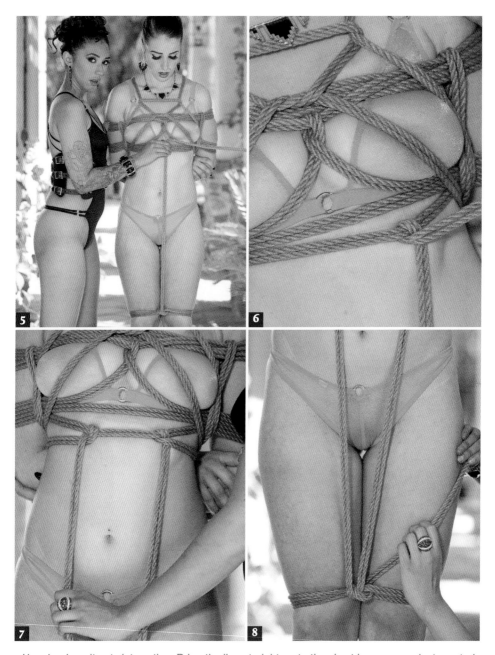

5 Here is where it gets interesting: Bring the line straight up to the chest harness you just created.
6 Come up and over the left side, then pull the rope around the back. **7** Come out on the right side and repeat the same hitch. Tip: Extra sex points if you make the hitches mirror each other.
8 Then drop down to your first set of wraps right above the knees. See how it makes a nice "V" at the top and narrows to a point at the knees? This will be crucial to the diamond pattern. Don't make the "V" tight. Even a little slack is fine, as it will tighten up in a moment.

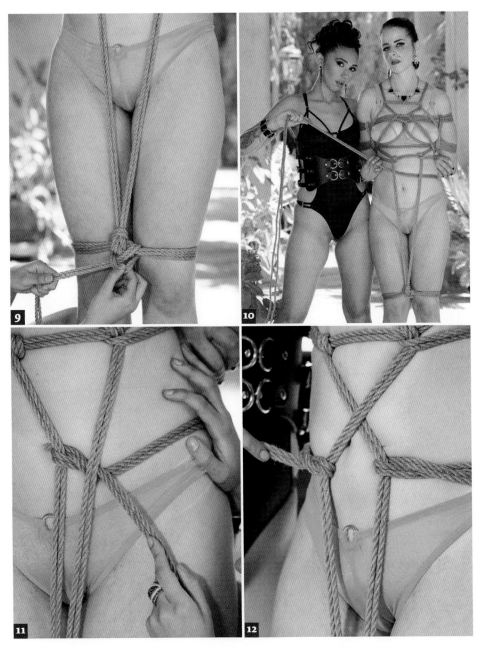

9 Secure the bottom with a hitch. 10 Here is the key: Come through the bottom and up the back, pick up a vertical line (any will do) in the back so you can come around to the front of the tummy, under the arm. Look at this picture closely. 11 Now, cross the first vertical line and go to the next one and come around it and back to the left side. 12 Come around the back and come out the right side, cross over to the other vertical line, make a wrap and start to pull it into position where they will cross each other.

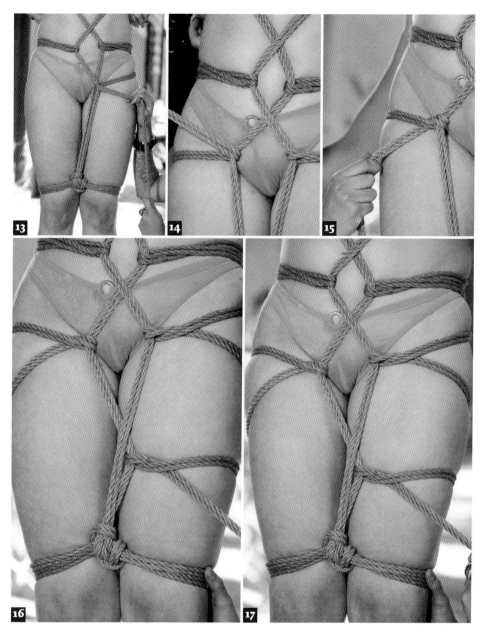

13 Then come around the back again, out the left side, cross over and pick up the opposing line. Can you see the pattern starting to emerge yet? **14** Tip: The key is to always pick up the line you left off with on the other side. **15** When you get over the hips, you want to start making it tighter. The more you pull the more it will accentuate the body part. **16** Down to the mid thigh. **17** If you notice, the pattern starts to bite into the skin. This is something that rope practitioners find very sexy: The compression of the skin, where you can not only see but feel it trapping your partner, making them an object of your desire.

18 Once you get it done, if you support them, they can walk in mincing steps to the couch where you can then start the next part of your sexy time, which is all up to you!

Open Leg Tie

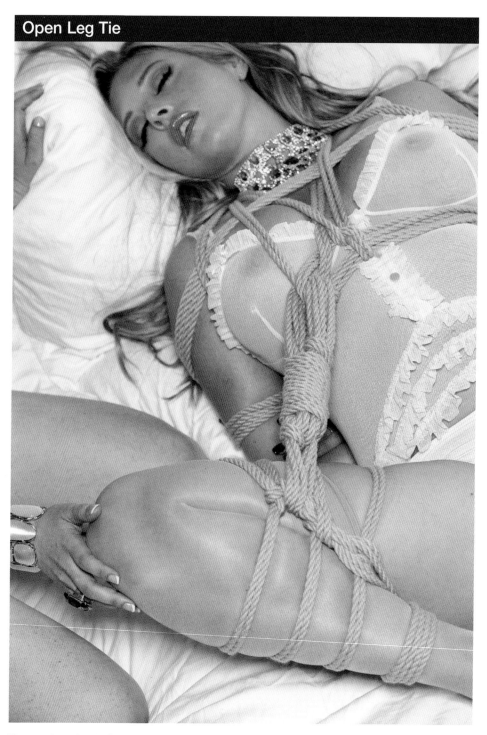

Here we have lovely Samantha and Vanessa who are going to show you how to tie your partner in a very comfortable spread-legged position.

1 It first begins with a very special chest harness which leaves a pretty HOTO knot in between the breasts. Capture their arms behind them in a single cuff tie around both wrists and bring the rope up and over. **2** Cross the rope between the breasts. **3** Then build two wraps above and below the breasts. **4** The back should look like this. **5** Finish the lower wrap and come back around the main line that is vertical.

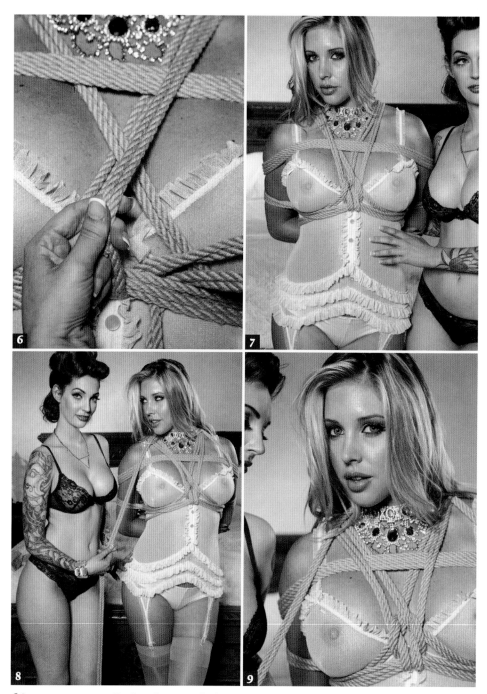

6 As you recross over the lines between the breasts, you should be alternating them. **7** Follow the lines, come up and over and then back down and you should have a very attractive HOTO knot right in the center. **8** Come up with a new length of rope tied in the back, over the shoulder and this time duck back through the armpit. **9** Here is a closer shot.

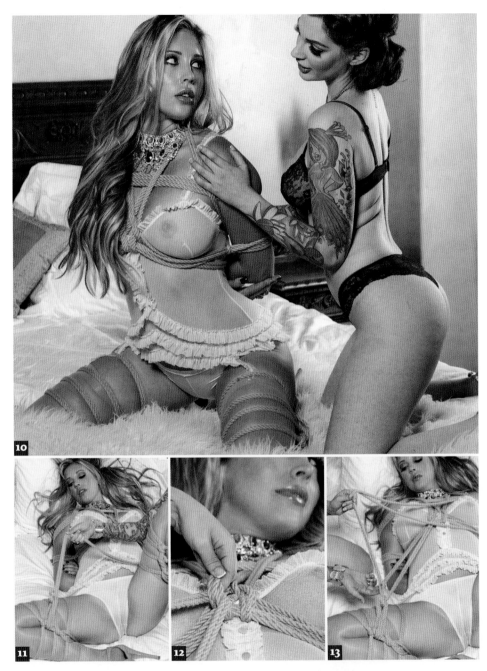

10 Now that you have them all tied up, let's get to the next stage. **11** With their arms behind them, lay them on something soft like a bed, it will be more comfortable. Start with a simple Futo tie around their leg and tie it off. **12** Take the free end left over from the leg and run it from the inside of the shin over a wrap and up through the center part of the chest tie. **13** Then back to the leg and through the loop you left when you started that tie.

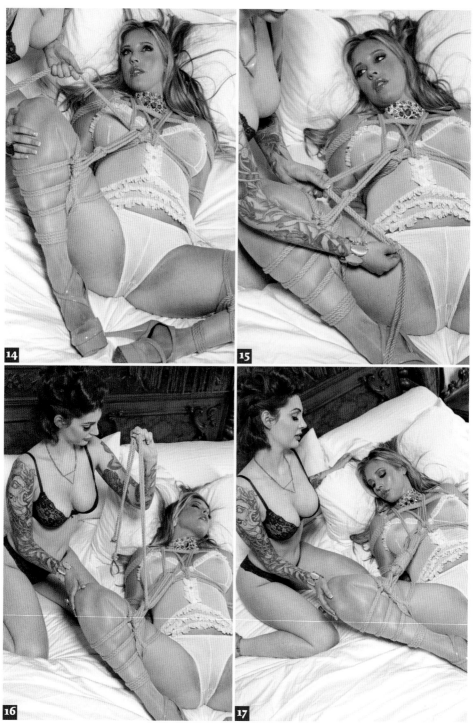

14 Passing through. **15** And once again back to where you started. **16** Now you have lots of rope to wind up the lines you just created. **17** And find a nice, pretty way to tie it off.

18 Here is a look at the final tie. You can repeat for the other leg.

Futo Leg Tie

"Futo" roughly translates to "chubby thigh," and this tie gets its sexiness from the rope pressing into the skin and making it look sexy. There are many types of thigh ties, but this one builds on a ladder pattern.

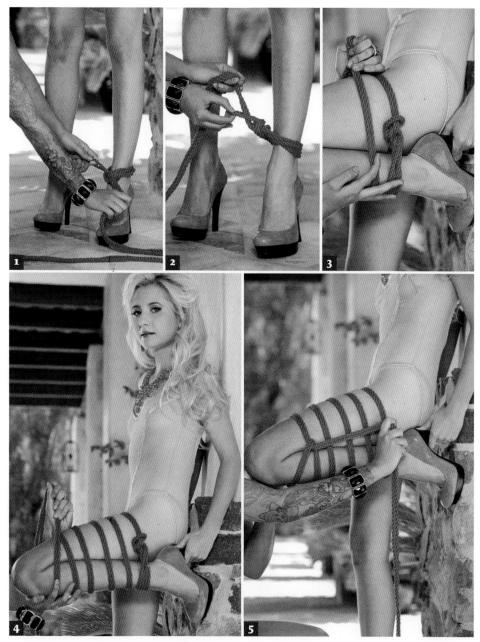

1 Start with a single-column tie around the ankle. **2** Make the knot good and secure and leave enough room so you can slip two fingers in behind the cuff. **3** Kerry here is lifting Odette's leg right up tight to her upper leg. It is important that you close the leg as much as possible. Begin wrapping around the thigh. The wraps don't have to be super tight. You will be able to fine-tune the tightness in the later part of the tie. **4** Create five wraps nice and even. **5** You are going to come back through the last wrap on the top and change direction and head back down the thigh.

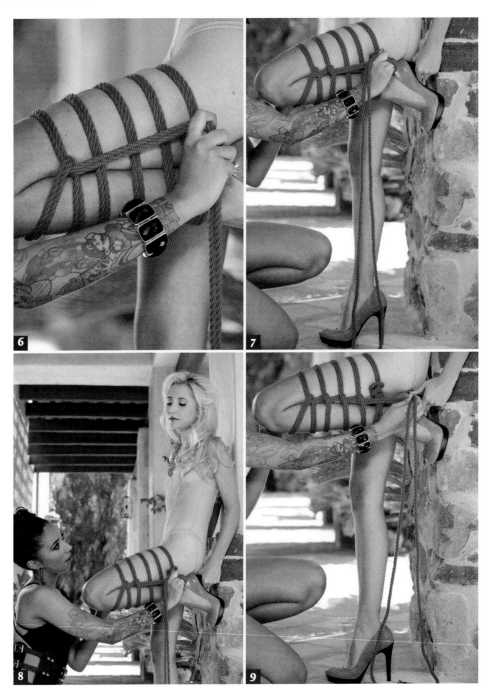

6 Here is a close-up. All the lines are nice and flat and smooth. **7** Go to the next lower wrap and tuck it under. **8** You are going to move all the way down the leg. Again, it doesn't have to be super tight, in fact it is best if it is only slightly snug right now. **9** Work your way all the way to the original wrap.

10 Here is where you can start fine-tuning the tightness. Come under the last wrap on the outside and pass it through to the inside of the thigh. **11** Now you are going to work your way up the thigh. **12** Doing the exact same crossover for each wrap until you get all the way to the top. **13** Where you will change direction and work your way downwards.

14 You should be running out of rope at this point. There are a few options but let's just end where we have rope, shall we? Come back under and through to your original side. **15** And start moving up the wraps once again. **16** Tip: The security of the tie doesn't necessarily come from being super tight, more from having a whole complete tie that encases the leg in a bent position. **17** Bonus Tip: Keep the wraps the same as you work back down so they look nice and neat.

18 Keeping the wraps nice and neat makes everything tie together beautifully. An alternative would be to use two different colors of rope. Have fun and be creative!

Strappado

The Strappado comes directly out of the history of Western bondage with rope artists like Paula Klaw and Lew Rubens. The Knotty Boys also have an elegant variation of this tie called the Dragonfly in their last book from Green Candy Press. I'd recommend that you try this out as well. These artists, born many decades apart, have used this tie for its elegant simplicity and effectiveness. If you want to try it, please be aware that both of you need to communicate even more so than with other ties. The pressure placed on the shoulders can be tailored to however you want it; it can be a nice easy stretch or it can be an endurance event. The Strappado is super sexy and can help the receiver to stretch and work up to more extreme ties down the road. It is an excellent piece to master as you move forward into intermediate tying. Please play safe.

1 Stand behind your partner and wrap the rope around their upper chest, over their shoulders.

2 You will initially start with the last four feet of rope that has the bight end (the folded over loop).

3 Wrap around the upper chest and shoulders twice. 4 Then tie the bight end so there is only about three inches left. Exactly like this. 5 Once it is secure you come up and over the right shoulder.

6 Then over the wraps and under the armpit and up the back.

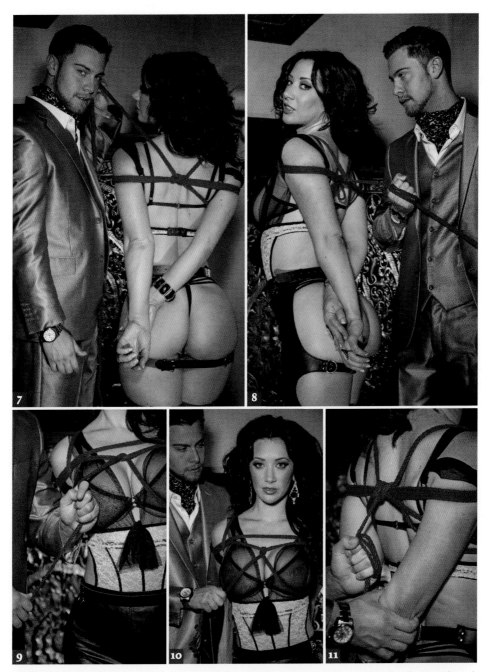

7 Make a simple wrap around the center. **8** Up over the other shoulder and under the armpit and tie it to the center again. **9** We want the front to be as pretty as the back so come up between the left arm and body, under the breast and up and over the bottom wrap on the front. **10** I like to create a little fish-tail twist. To do so, simply make a twist as you pass over the rope, then bring the line down under the breast. **11** You should finish off the line in the back like this.

12 You've now created a foundation for the rest of the tie to be anchored from. **13** Now you are going to start the wraps that travel down the arms. **14** Wrap above the elbows on the meat of the arm, not down where the bone comes to the surface. This is more comfortable. **15** See how we have all the lines nice and neat without any twists? That is how you should be doing it.

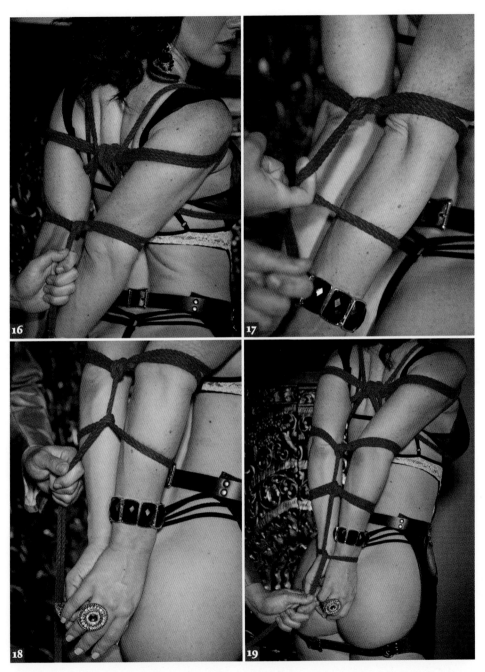

16 A nice simple hitch around the entire wrap, both front and back, will secure the elbows. Listen to the person being tied. They will let you know how tight they are comfortable with in this position. **17** Now drop the line down past the elbows, onto the meat of the forearm. **18** Wrap around, come under the vertical line and then go back the way you came. **19** Finish it off with a hitch, pulling both the front and back wrap snug, then drop a line down to the wrists.

20 Do the exact same thing around the wrists, with two wraps, or four lines to secure them.
21 Now for a little flourish and style! You may find you have extra rope left over. The simplest and most creative thing you can do is start wrapping it back up the vertical lines. **22** All the way to the top. **23** If their arms start to become tired but they don't want to have the bondage removed, they can gently bend at the elbows and stretch themselves. Don't do it for them; support them but don't do the stretching for them.

24 There we go, nice and pretty and waiting for some playtime!

Ruben's Gunslinger Hip Harness

Lew Rubens is best noted for his development of this tie in the West. He was the first one I know of in the online world to be using it as early as the late 1990s. It is a great tie, secure and easy. And it looks utterly fantastic.

1 Get behind your sexy partner and put a loop around their middle, down past the hip bones. The strength of this tie comes with the rope anchored firmly on the hips, not up on the tummy. Run the free end through just like this. 2 Go around the body once more and then back through the original loop. Knot it off and then come down the leg and around the thigh and back through the vertical line. It is a little tricky to keep the tension on the rope at all times but it will help you to achieve a much cleaner-looking harness when it's done. 3 Make another wrap around the thigh and come back through the original loop. 4 It should look just like this. 5 Knot it off with a simple cinch, just like this. 6 Now that it is cinched off, we are going to build the handle. Take the excess and start wrapping up the vertical rope.

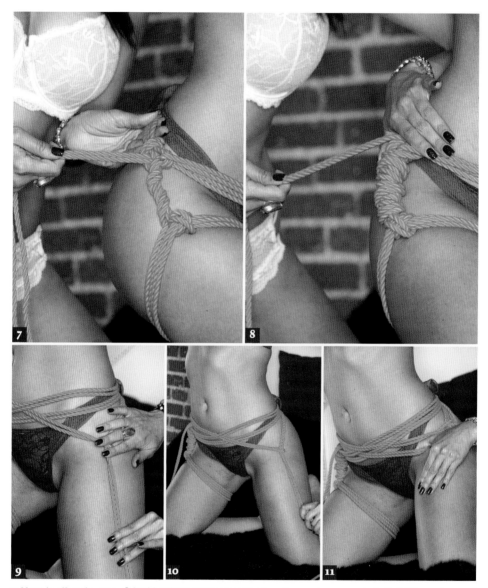

7 Knot it off at the top. **8** And begin to wrap over the handle you have created. Build it up nice and thick and find a nice neat way to use up any extra rope and knot it off. **9** Here is where it is going to become even prettier. This next step is a mirror of the first part only on the other side and with a small addition. When you make the loop around the body, in the front, you will create a small weaving that will add extra visual impact. Pull the loop around the body like before but this time tuck it under just one of the bands previously created before you pull it through the loop and head down the leg. **10** See how pretty this is going to look? **11** As you make another wrap, tuck it though the front, alternating the lines until you get a nice weave. This will be good practice for more advanced weaving in the book.

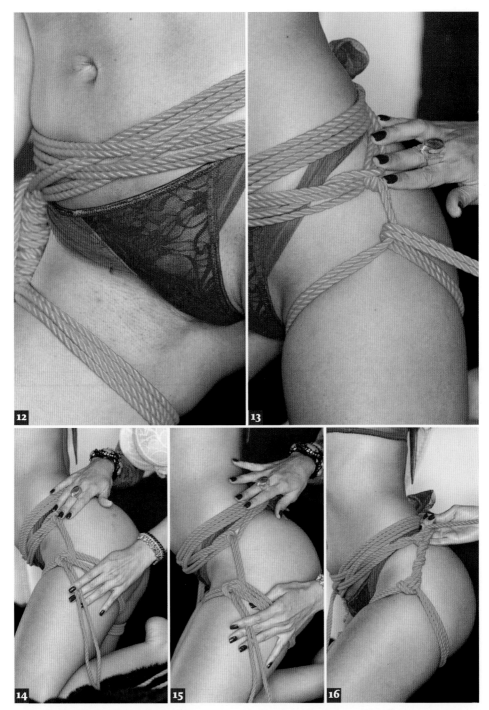

12 Gorgeous. **13** Just like the other side, it is time to make the thigh wrap. **14** Make a wrap around the thigh and cinch it after two wraps. **15** Again, like the other side, start building the handle. **16** Wrap all the way up the handle, and when you have used up your extra rope, cinch it off.

17 Almost done!

18 Now they are ready for you to tell them what to do! The handles are perfect for doggie-style sexy time.

Chapter Seven

Difficult Intermediate Ties

The ties in this chapter will be the most difficult ones that we'll deal with in this book, so I've put them in order of skill level. It may take you a little while to conquer the Leg Weave and the Messy Futo, but don't be disheartened; these are incredibly skillful ties and you will eventually get there; remember, it's not a race!

It's important to remember that if a tie is more challenging for the rigger, it's also more challenging for the bunny. As always, safety is of primary importance. If your partner isn't feeling up to it, then try something that you know well and that's easier on the mind and body, or pick it up another time.

Facing Page: Two playful little kitties, all bound up in rope. The possibilities are endless.

Daisy Chain Up the Body

The Daisy Chain is a fun and playful way to make bands of rope up or down the body. It looks sexier than just wrapping around the body and you can find a small variation, the Lightning Bolt, later in this chapter.

1 Start with the requisite wrap around the body, down below the hips, and bring the free end through. **2** After you cinch the knot by the belly button, turn them around and pull the rope up between their bum cheeks. **3** Then come up and over the waist rope and give it a snug pull. This sets the rope firmly between the cheeks and lets them know you mean business! **4** Cinch the knot.

5 Then go back the way you came, between the cheeks, legs and out to the front again. **6** Pull it up and over the waist rope, just a loop, not the whole rope. **7** And cinch it off. Bonnie here makes it look so good! **8** Now put a wrap around the body up above the belly button on the torso.

9 Instead of pulling the whole free end of the rope through, just pull a loop. It is important to keep this rope snug as you work so the Daisy Chain doesn't fall apart. **10** Here is a close-up shot. **11** The only tricky part is making continuous loops in the middle and holding it firmly while you do so it doesn't fall apart. **12** Here is a close-up. **13** See? From the front you will just keep pulling a short three-inch loop through, then going back around the body and pulling another short three-inch loop through.

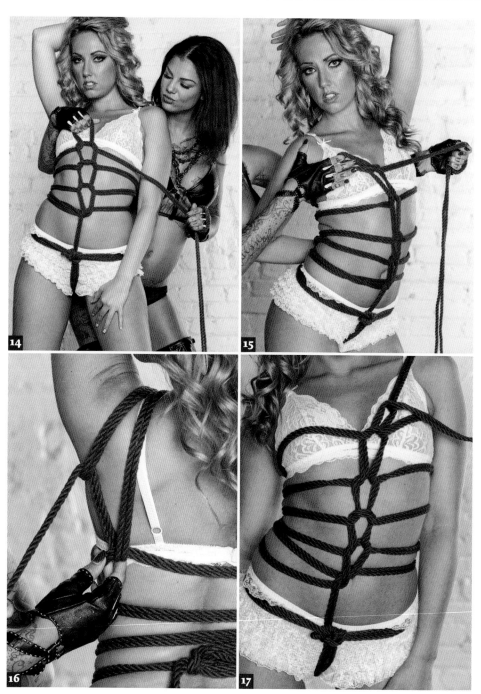

14 And work all the way up the body, past the breasts. **15** There are a few different options for how to end this. Demonstrated on Sarah is a one-shoulder cinch. Keeping the rope snug as you tie, take the last loop and pull the free end through it and head over the shoulder to the back. **16** Over the shoulder and find a bottom wrap to tie it to. **17** The front should look like this.

18 Now they are all yours. Have fun!

Hishi with Arms Crossed in Front

A "hishi" tie refers to the repeating pattern of diamonds or triangles across the body, wrapping around your partner like a net, capturing them in your web. It looks hot and complicated, but it's really about following a pattern and keeping the hitches neat and clean. There are only two distinct parts: The arms and then the chest.

1 Start with a single-column tie around the wrist, available in my previous book *Bondage Basics*.

2 Have your partner cross their hand to the opposite hip and then pull the rope around their back.

3 Then capture the other wrist so they look like this with the same rope.

4 Come up over the left shoulder. **5** Over the chest and around the back, right over the triceps area on their arm. Then make a Munter Hitch right over the shoulder blade. **6** Confused yet? Hang in there, you will see with this next step where we are going with this tie! Once you get the hitch on the back complete, cross over the right shoulder and where the rope crosses right below her neck, Kerry is going to put another Munter Hitch right there. Keep it lower and away from their throat please. **7** Travel over the opposite shoulder you just tied, around the back, make another hitch over the left shoulder blade and then come over the left shoulder and make a hitch in the rope you just left on the chest. Now you should see the pattern starting to emerge.

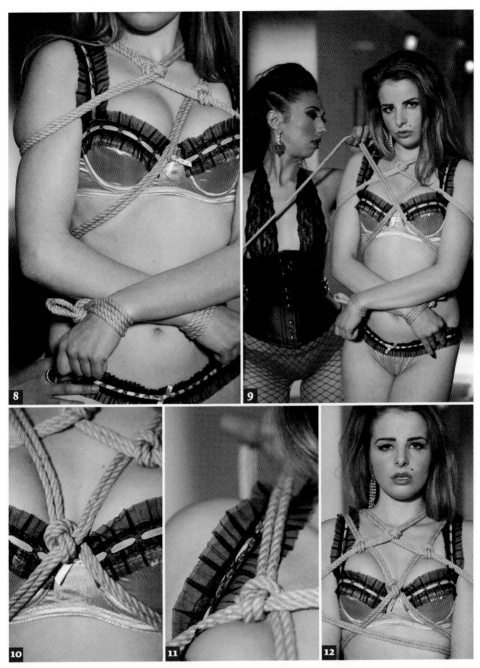

8 Instead of going over the arm with this next step, you will travel along and pass between the arm and the body, making the rope snug but not overly tight. **9** Come straight around the back and up between the left arm and torso and cross between the breasts. **10** Make a pretty Munter Hitch exactly as you see here. **11** Then rise up to the next intersecting rope and do another. **12** It should really be coming along. You are almost done!

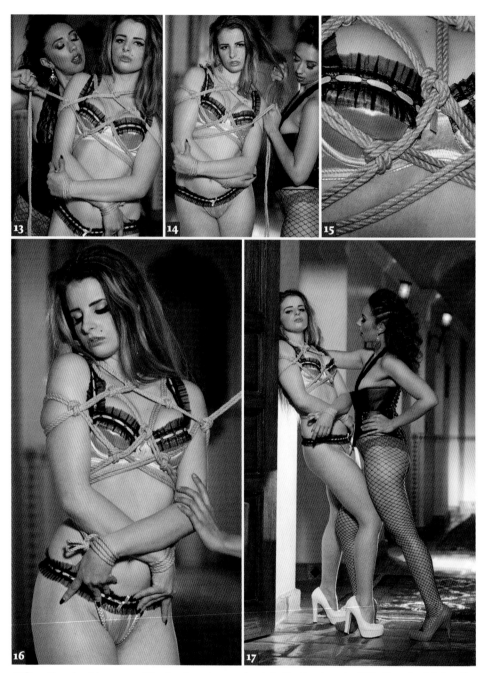

13 Over the shoulder, around the back and come back to the front again. This time the hitch will go on top of the outside of the arm. **14** Everything should be symmetrical on both sides of the body. Whatever you do on one side, you will copy for the other side. **15** Here is a close-up of the process. **16** Finishing off, over the left arm, make a hitch and then travel to the back. **17** Secure the tie in the back and now Kerry can boss Blair around!

18 The entire tie needs to be firm but not overly tight. The security comes from the multiple wraps and the beauty comes from the repeating pattern.

Lightning Bolt

This tie builds on the foundation that you learned with the Daisy Chain and requires you to have a hard point in the ceiling or top frame of your fabulous four-poster bed. If you don't know what I mean by this, stop right there. You should have experience with knowing what is a secure hard point and what is not. Go learn. Quick. We'll wait.

1 Start with a two-column tie around the ankles and leave a large loop on one end that we are going to use in a moment. **2** Have your honey lift her legs straight up. Underneath the suspension point, run the rope up through it and back down and through the loop, creating a basic pulley (you WERE paying attention in high school physics, weren't you?). **3** Once it is through, pull straight up, stretch those legs out until it's nice and comfortable and the legs are straight. The legs have to be straight for this to look pretty. **4** Here is a closer look at how it should pass through before it goes up and holds the legs up.

5 When you go back through the hard point, you have a system where you can pull on the end and it will help raise the legs. **6** Now Bonnie has Idelsy's legs up in the air and ready for the next step. **7** It starts with the high heel shoes. Let's enjoy this gratuitous shot of Bonnie appreciating them in her own way, shall we? **8** Make a simple Lark's Head knot and slip it over the heel, push it up as far as you can. This is the anchor point for the tie.

9 It should look just like this at this point. **10** Like the Daisy Chain tie, you are going to make a series of loops that are all interconnected down the leg so it is important to keep tension on the rope so it doesn't fall apart. Wrap around the ankles and pull about three inches of loop through. **11** Just like this. **12** As you work down the leg, the difference with this tie is you will pull the loop through but keep the tension on the bias, so it lies diagonally as it travels down the legs.

13 You accomplish this by pulling the loop over to one side of the leg, then the next one way over the other way. It looks funny at first until you really start building a pattern. **14** Just like this.

15 Here is a close-up of how the loop should look as you build each wrap around the leg.

16 When you get to the knees, make a wrap above and then below them. You want your rope to be on the fleshy part of the body, not the bony parts. **17** Keep it up until you get to the crotch.

18 The way you finish this tie is by passing the free end through the very last loop and burying it under the bum as you bring the rope up and wrap around the lower part of the waist.

Nouveau Hogtie

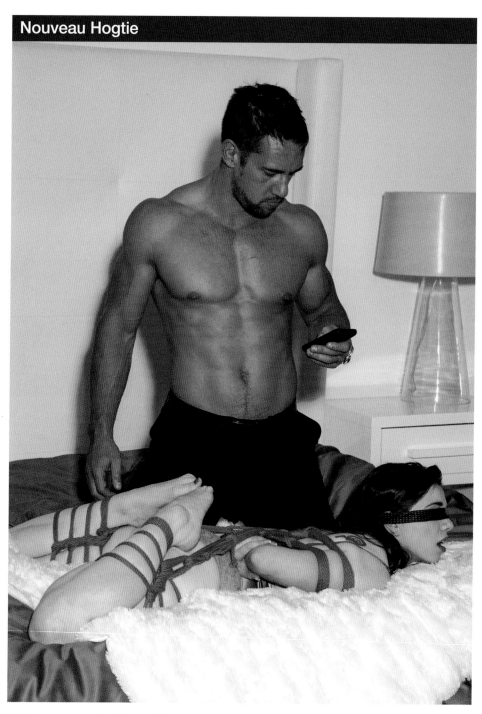

This is a more comfortable variation of the classic hogtie and it also solves a super sexy problem with a standard hogtie that you will see at the end. You should already know a one-column tie, a Futo and a chest harness since this uses all of them to pull it together.

1 For this demonstration the models are using a bed for the main reason that it has little give, and is more flexible on Sarah Hunter's diaphragm. Please don't tie your partner like this on a hard floor. You need to have a chest harness already built on your partner. **2** Johnny likes to use a blindfold to build anticipation. **3** Build a Futo on both legs separately. **4** Take a third piece of rope and tuck the middle part under the mid-thigh wrap. **5** Pass it through twice.

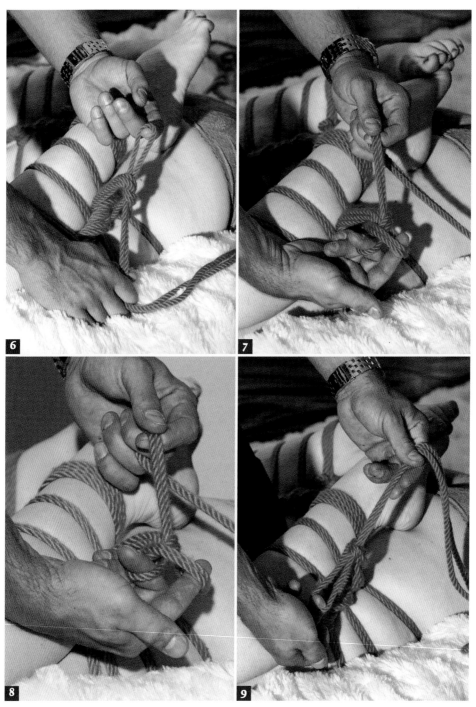

6 And then start to build one-column tie around the thigh wraps. Keep it loose. **7** Make one more knot to secure the wrap as a large loop around the thigh wraps. **8** Here is a closer look. **9** Pull it tight to set the knot firmly in place.

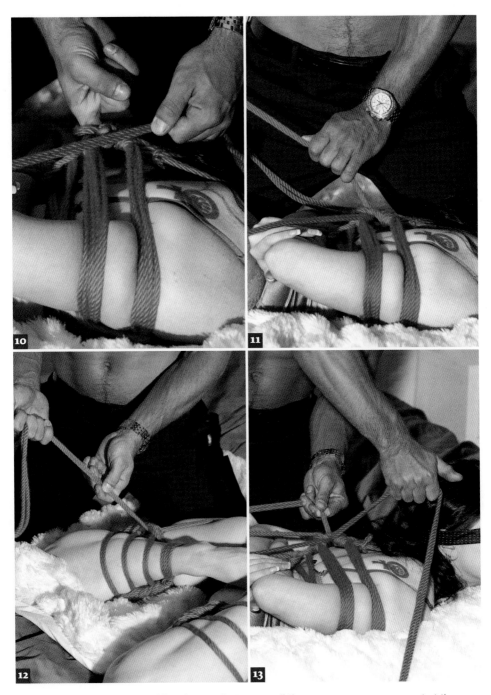

10 Now, take the free end and head up to the torso, pull the wraps up so you can get at the vertical stem easier. **11** Around the vertical stem and out the other side. **12** Come to the other leg on the outside and run the rope through the mid part. **13** And then head back up to the chest harness, and trace the last line, all the way back.

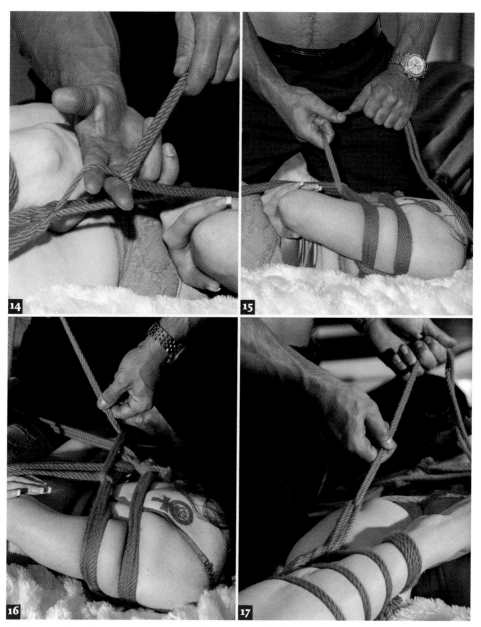

14 Here is where the magic happens. In a hogtie, tying it all together nice and tight is essential in the whole piece. The way we do this is by picking up the loop you left idle on the first leg, just like this. **15** Then come up to one of the chest wraps on the back and come under. This will provide you with a rudimentary pulley which you can tighten in slow increments. **16** When you get the legs tightened exactly to where you and your partner want, you can move across to the other side with a hitch. **17** And head down to the leg and use up extra rope by winding it around to make it look pretty.

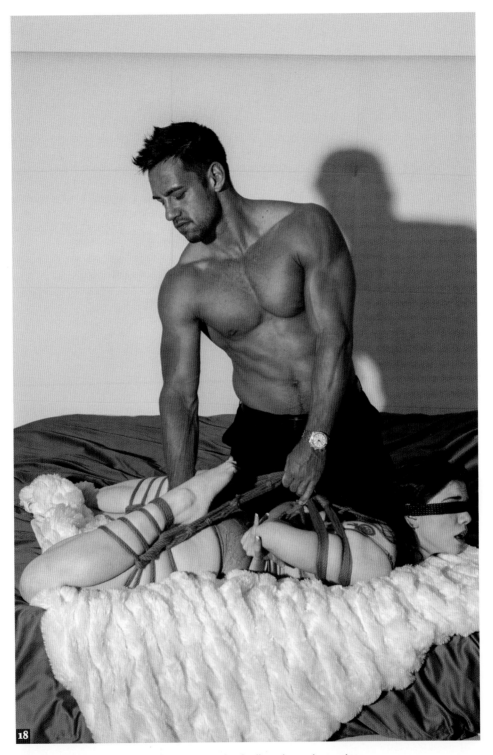

18 If you drop your phone, make sure you check all nooks and crannies.

Leg Weave

This is one of the most challenging ties in this book, but it is also the most decorative. I have saved it for later in the book to inspire you to reach out into your creative spirit as you finish this book and move onwards to creating your own style of rope bondage.

1 Start with a simple waist tie and lock it off. Then stretch the rope down the inside of the leg.

2 Make two wraps exactly like you see here: Mid thigh and mid calf. 3 Then around the ankle.

4 Here is a close-up.

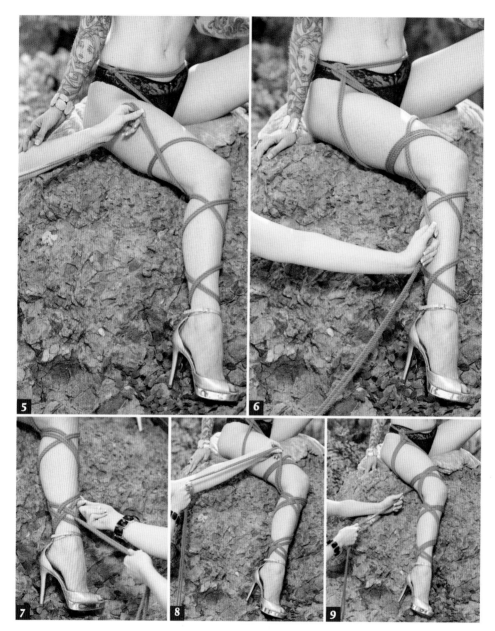

5 The strength of this tie lies in the pattern and how close you stick to it with each twist and turn. Make two more winds so that you now have rope that makes little *X*s on the leg as you travel upwards. **6** Go all the way up to the waist, around it and back down, tracing the lines as you go. **7** Just like with other weaving, you will start to alternate over/under as you start crossing lines. Take your time, there is no need to rush. **8** The pattern should be emerging now as you trace the lines of the rope up and back down the leg. **9** Make sure you push the lines close together as you weave over/under to keep them neat and clean.

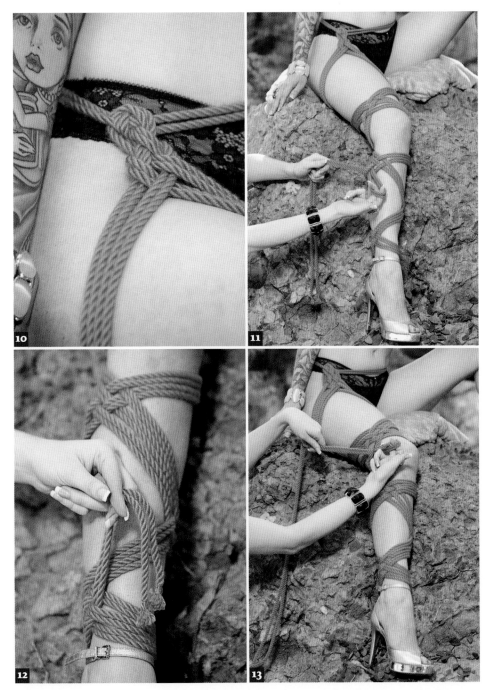

10 When you come up to the waist, you can even put some weaves into the turnaround point.

11 I always find when I am weaving that pulling the loop of the rope through is easier than trying to push the end of the rope through. **12** As we get to the end it will be time to add more rope.

13 The more wraps you add, the more visual interest you create.

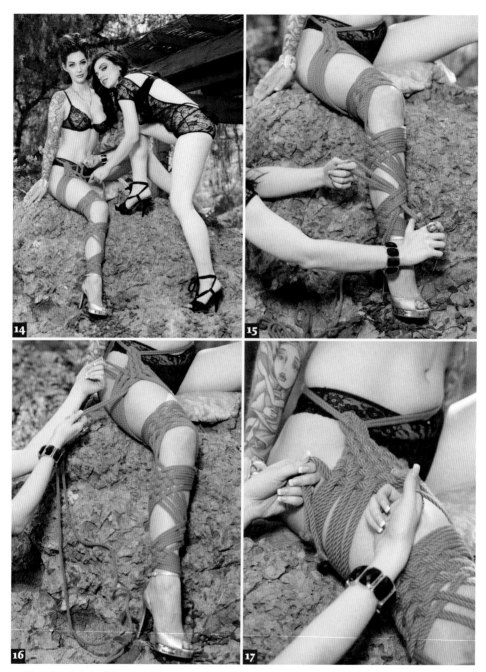

14 Here Sarah is building up the turnaround point which starts to look like a super sexy rope garter. **15** We have about five lines built up and that is about the number we are going to stop at. **16** Now we have four nice wide bands that wrap seductively around the leg. It looks awesome with the high heels. **17** To finish off this tie, I like to use up the extra rope on the top part, around the turnaround point and then find a place to tuck the ends.

18 Beautiful. Simply beautiful.

Messy Futo

This Futo assumes you have spent time learning the simpler version of the Futo that is in this book. In this particular tie, Candle is partially suspended by her wrists but most of her weight is on her knees. It is a wildly artistic variation of the Futo and will give you the chance to start to express yourself with rope. Once you've mastered this, you're more than ready to go forth and let yourself go wild (creatively speaking, that is).

1 To start, your partner should be in the kneeling position or even lying on a bed. **2** Start with a single-column tie around the ankle. **3** Now Johnny is going to start wrapping the tie around the upper thigh by the crease. **4** Go all the way around the folded leg. Go up to the knee and then all the way back.

5 Instead of nice, even wraps, make several more and change the angle of them as you go as you can see here. 6 Wrap all the way down the leg. Every line should feel intentional rather than haphazard. 7 When you get to the knee, put a twist hitch in it like this so you can start working back towards the body. 8 Be sure to keep everything neat and tidy here, as it will help you later on.

9 As Johnny starts tying down the thigh, even though the overall wraps appear chaotic, the hitches he is tying are clean and not twisted.

10 And we continue to repeat all the way up the leg. **11** The way this becomes more artistic is to skip a few lines rather than tying to every single one. **12** Make sure the ones you do tie are neat and tidy with a good hitch. This will pull all the elements together. **13** Just like this. See how the angled ones are skipped in the tie but still bring a visual interest to the overall piece.

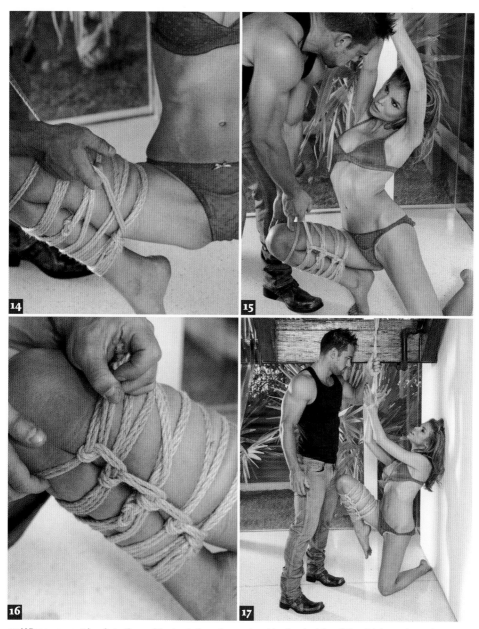

14 When you get back to the ankle, tuck it under and out to the inside of the thigh and continue with your hitches. **15** Build it all the way up to the knee and finish off the tie someplace orderly and tidy. **16** Tuck the ends in so they aren't unsightly. Neatness is a virtue! **17** Your success at a messy Futo will depend largely on how you decide to play with the elements of design. Here Johnny has used the extra lines that have been skipped, coupled with the neatness of the hitches, to give it an intentional look. Whenever you bring your rope bondage art out of patterns and into the realm of art, it is because you have made intentional choices.

18 If you're like me, and you like symmetry, you'll want to do the other leg too!

Chapter Eight

Becoming a Bona Fide Rope Bondage Obsessive

If you're anything like me, rope will have started to take over your life by now. Some people (apparently) can keep bondage as a little hobby, a folly, something that they do a couple of times a week and don't think about in between. Well, frankly, I don't know any of these people and they sound boring anyway. I know the obsessives; the ones who just can't stop.

If you've been tantalized and semi-scandalized by the ties in this book and you're well on your way to mastering them, you're most likely turning into one of us (one of us, one of us...). It will start to take over your every waking minute; there's no point resisting, so you might as well go with it.

Going further into rope bondage doesn't just mean continuing on your education; it also means investing time and energy into doing all the basics better. It also means branching out into the community, in order to be inspired and to contribute to the fantastic culture of bondage as a whole. Here are some things I'd recommend doing.

Facing Page: Bound legs, hot rope, sexy heels. Is there anything better?

Teach your sub to tie other bunnies and you'll have a world of fun.

Invest in Better Materials

I've said this many times in my previous books, but it's worth saying again as it's something I very much believe in; support artisan designers and makers of bondage goods. When we're starting out we often go for the cheapest materials, unsure of whether we'll really make the best of the financial investment; no one wants to lay out hundreds of dollars for something that might lie mostly unused in the bottom drawer after a few weeks. That's understandable.

However, when you're sure that your love of bondage isn't going away, it's time to invest in things that are better; better for you, better for the environment, better for the community as a whole. There are some incredibly talented and innovative makers of rope, and these producers, as they share your passion, will always craft their materials with your needs in mind. A product created by someone who knows exactly what it will be used for will be perfectly crafted to those uses. Producers of high-quality rope have years of experience under their belts and have spent decades honing their craft. Support them if you can. Buying from small manufacturers helps to create a larger industry; these manufacturers can employ other people and their company can grow. Buy things made in your home country if you can, with extra points if you buy local. If you purchase your materials from people who love rope, they will be able to make better and better products and your life will improve and everyone's better off in the long run, trust me.

Learn to Love Your Rope

I've already shown you how to treat your rope and prep it for use, but as you invest in more expensive types, you'll need to know how to properly look after it, to ensure that its quality remains high over time. This will become something of a ritual for you, and might even become something that settles you and brings you gently back down to earth after a play session. All good things.

As your rope collection grows, you'll get used to coiling and storing it with a little more care. You spent a lot of money on it, so you might as well put the effort into putting it away correctly. Coil it well and store it in a cool, dry, dark spot, somewhere that won't make your mother ask questions when she comes round for tea.

What with all the sweat and fluids and hormones flying around during a play session, your rope will become dirty over time (much like your mind). In the interests of hygiene (and not scaring away a play partner with your stinky rope), you should wash your rope when you think it needs it. Your different types of rope will each have to be washed in a different way; we'll discuss these below. Don't wash different colored ropes together, as they might still have some dye in them and the colors will bleed, just like that pair of red underwear that snuck into the washing machine that one time and turned all your work shirts cerise.

While it's preferable to hand wash your rope, you can also toss it into the washing machine if you prefer. For nylon rope, coil it into a loose figure eight and place it inside a pillowcase before putting it into your washing machine; this will stop the rope from getting caught on anything, and helps to preserve the quality. Wash in a cold water cycle, or on a delicate setting. Let the rope drip-dry for an hour, then place into your dryer on a low setting until it's nearly done. Stretch it out. Put it back into the dryer for the final period. If you don't have a dryer, it's fine to air-dry your rope.

Hemp, cotton, silk and bamboo rope can be washed in the same way, but should be left to air-dry. You may need to periodically stretch the rope through the drying process to keep it supple. When hemp rope (and only hemp) is dry, you should oil it using a small amount of baby or jojoba oil, or made-for-purpose rope oil. Don't use oil on other types of rope.

Like a good, old, comfy pair of Levi's, rope becomes more supple, but also weaker, with extended use—and with excessive washing. While it's a good idea to wash your rope from time to time, each wash will age it somewhat, so try to keep it moderately regular but not too often. You should be extremely careful about using older ropes for weight-bearing ties and suspensions, as they can lose their strength with overuse. Err on the side of caution always when it comes to suspension ties and the ropes used. Depending on the situation and how much use my rope will see and in what environment (dirty, sexy warehouse or clean bedroom?) I wash my rope about once a year as a rule of thumb.

Jute rope should only be washed if it has come into contact with bodily fluids like blood or semen, as water will weaken its fibers. To wash jute, place it into a pot of boiling water for about fifteen minutes, then allow it to cool before handling as it will be incredibly hot. Dry it under tension, otherwise it will shrink. As we've mentioned blood, I should also say this: Be aware that the transfer of blood can create a safety risk; get yourself tested for STDs regularly and maintain your sexual safety.

You can dye your own cotton rope, and I recommend doing it at least once. It's a great skill to learn and will save you money in the long run, as you can buy plain cotton rope for less money and dye it to your preferred color. There's something both fun and intense about this process that makes you understand the physical makeup of your rope even better.

Learn from Others

Depending on your relationship situation, you may be open to exploring bondage with a number of partners. This can be platonic or sexual; how you do it, or whether you do it at all, is up to you. However, whether you're a rigger or a bunny, playing with other people will allow you to learn from them and appreciate the unique styles that everyone brings to bondage. If your relationship situation doesn't lend itself to playing with others, then workshops or classes can be a fantastic resource for you. Learning works best in a group setting, so if you spend time around others who are more skilled than you, it gives you the chance to get better, rather than learning from a group that is of your same skill level. There are enough rope bondage conferences around to cater to everyone's skill levels; a fan-

Chest ties always let a bunny know who's boss.

tastic one is the Florida Intensive Rope Experience (F.I.R.E.) which is a three-day convention in Orlando every August, bringing together some of the best rope bondage talent from around the world to share their knowledge and experience. I highly recommend you attend some of these types of conferences—they're a lot of fun!

As mentioned earlier, I highly recommend seeking out a mentor who can guide, nurture and encourage you as you go beyond what's shown in this book and even in classes and workshops. A good mentor will be able to understand your goals and strengths as well as your fears and weaknesses, and will offer a path to greater success with rope. They will mold you into a fantastic bondage specialist in their own image. There's nothing better.

Become a Pillar of the Bondage Community

For a lot of people, this is a bigger step than it seems. In the bedroom, we can be whoever we want to be—and a rope bunny or a rigger might have a completely different persona in a scene than the one they have in "real life." BDSM and bondage act as escapes from normal life for many people, so to bring that love out onto the street or into a pub or restaurant can seem like a daunting task.

Have you ever heard the phrase "there's strength in numbers"? You might be afraid that people will think you strange for liking to be hogtied and flogged senseless—but you won't feel so strange when you're surrounded by dozens of other kinksters who love the same sort of thing. Getting out into the bondage community can not only give you the confidence to be who you really want to be in the bondage world; it can open up new relationships that can take you places you never expected that you would go.

For instance, you might be exploring bondage with a long-term partner, but with a vague idea that you'd both like to involve someone else in your scenes—just not in your life. Attending a munch (a meet-up for kinky folks) can introduce you to many other people with similar interests, and you might find the perfect play partner, one who wants to be bound and contorted and enjoy you both but isn't looking to become involved in a relationship or anything at all romantic. Perhaps both you and your partner are looking for play partnerships outside of your primary relationship; the chances are that you will meet a few people who are looking for something similar, and yet others who can offer advice on how to make such a situation a success.

If you're an unattached bondage fan, these meet-ups can be a fantastic place to meet new riggers or bunnies with whom you can explore your love of rope. If you're not looking for anyone to engage in scenes with, then don't worry! Many other kinksters just go along to these events to meet like-minded folks and make friends, far away from any implication of future playing. The bondage community is supportive, understanding and nonjudgmental, so you shouldn't be afraid to get out there, no matter what you're looking for.

I'm incredibly lucky that my passion has become my life; I get to travel all over the world teaching, rigging, photographing and writing, and I've had all sorts of gorgeous things beneath my rope, in front of my camera and reading my books (yep, that includes you). But even if you are stuck in your home city working 9-5, with only your evenings and your weekends free to explore your rope passion, there are still many ways that you can open your life up and bring bondage into it in a real and meaningful way. And before you know it, you'll be a bona fide rope bondage obsessive just like the rest of us!

Facing Page: An exhausted bunny is a happy bunny. Don't disappoint her!

Glossary

Aftercare

A period of physical and mental care for all participants following a play session. In bondage, this involves tending to abrasions.

Arnica cream

A type of ointment used to soothe muscles, reduce inflammation and heal wounds. Perfect for tending to any play injuries.

Bondage tape

A reuseable, self-adhesive plastic material intended for use in erotic bondage. Should always be applied flat, not twisted.

Carabiners

A coupling link with a safety closure. Used for rock climbing, but also extensively used in bondage.

Consent

Positive, unambiguous, and voluntary agreement to engage in specific sexual activity throughout a sexual encounter. Must be sought and given throughout every play session.

Corset tie

A beautiful tie which goes across the chest, around the breasts then encases the torso, much like a corset.

Cuff tie

A multiple-wrap tie that encases the wrist.

Decorative ties

Ties meant purely for aesthetic purposes, and not to be used for sex.

Double-column tie

A tie that binds together two "columns" of the body; e.g., the arms or the lower legs.

Ebi tie

A.k.a. the "shrimp" tie, this tie attaches the legs to a body tie, forcing the body into a bent-over position.

Facing Page: Take your time with intricate ties. After all, the view ain't so bad.

Futo tie
A leg binding tie that folds the leg and binds the calf to the thigh. Loosely translated from Japanese, it means "chubby thigh."

Hishi tie
A decorative chest tie in a diamond pattern.

Hitch
A common knot used to connect a rope to a cylindrical object.

Hogtie
A tie that binds together a submissive's wrists and ankles behind their back, leaving them deliciously vulnerable.

Lark's Head knot
A.k.a. the Cow Hitch, this knot is used to attach rope to an object. A common knot used in many arenas.

Leg spreaders
A metal or wooden bar with ankle cuffs at each end, designed to keep legs open and ankles apart.

Limb restraint
Any sort of physical object that limits the movement of an arm or leg.

Manila
A traditional type of rope made from manila hemp. Unsuitable for most bondage as it is tough and doesn't knot well.

Morpheous' Rope Bondage Extravaganza
The world's largest, single night rope bondage exhibit.

Munter hitch
A hitch that is used in rope bondage that wraps around another rope that is decorative and offers a small anchor point.

Nerve location
Where nerves are on the body. An essential set of information for any rigger.

Polypropelyene
The cheap, tough material used to make inexpensive ropes in your local DIY store. Scratchy and painful and not for bondage use.

Prayer tie
A tie that brings the arms together in front of the body, making the hands appear as if praying.

Reef knot
Right over left and left over right. Not a good knot for bondage due to its tendency to capsize on itself under strain.

Safety shears

A set of sturdy shears that can cut through rope. An essential part of any bondage kit. Don't play without them.

Safeword

A term that stops all BDSM and bondage play, no matter what. Should be something not often said in playtime.

Sisal

A tough rope material that tends to splinter and doesn't knot well. Best avoided for bondage play.

St. Andrew's Cross

An X-shaped construction used to restrain ankles, wrist and waist all at once.

Sub drop

The "comedown" feeling that can follow an intense play session. Usually experienced by the submissive partner.

Subspace

That magical, ethereal place where nothing exists beyond your immediate sensory experiences. The holy grail for submissives.

Suspension

A form of bondage where the bound person is hung from a suspension point overhead.

Suspension ring

A thick metal ring hung from a structure or ceiling to facilitate suspension bondage. Always buy good quality ones.

The Connection

The most important part of any play session. The electricity that moves between a rigger and bunny.

Top drop

Similar to sub drop; a "comedown" feeling sometimes experienced after play, but this time by the Dominant partner.

Vacuum bed

A restriction device created by sheets of latex stretched over a frame. Air is removed by a vacuum, and the individual becomes immobile.

Weight distribution

The manner in which a person's weight is shared between weight-bearing parts of a tie during suspension.

Wraps

Created when rope winds around a part of the body.

Resources

Suggested Reading

■ *A Guide to Sexual Misery*, by Bernhard Ludwig (Vienna: Uberreuter, 2005).

■ *Bound to Be Free: The SM Experience*, by Charles Moser and JJ Madeson (London: Bloomsbury Academic, 1998).

■ *Bondage for Sex*, by Chanta Rose (San Francisco: BDSM Press, 2005).

■ *Erotic Bondage Handbook*, by Jay Wiseman (San Francisco: Greenery Press, 2000).

■ *How to be Kinkier: More Adventures in Adult Playtime*, by Morpheous (San Francisco: Green Candy Press, 2012).

■ *How to be Kinky: A Beginner's Guide to BDSM*, by Morpheous (San Francisco: Green Candy Press, 2008).

■ *On the Safe Edge: A Manual for SM Play*, by Trevor Jacques (Toronto: Whole SM Publishing, 1993).

■ *The Seductive Art of Japanese Bondage*, by Midori and Craig Morey (San Francisco: Greenery Press, 2002).

■ *Two Knotty Boys Back on the Ropes*, by Two Knotty Boys (San Francisco: Green Candy Press, 2010).

■ *Two Knotty Boys Showing You the Ropes*, by Two Knotty Boys (San Francisco: Green Candy Press, 2006).

■ *Wild Side Sex: The Book of Kink*, by Midori (Los Angeles: Daedalus Publishing, 2013).

■ Lew Rubens, though he doesn't have a book published, has been a great influence on both me and my style. I highly recommend that you check out his work at lewrubensproductions.zenfolio.com.

Facing Page: Let your imagination soar; let your rope work become intricate and gorgeous.

Rope Suppliers

There are a growing number of excellent artisan rope makers, and I highly recommend looking at who works in your area; buy local! Rope makers are talented, passionate, and make quality products, so support the artists that share your passion rather than buying cheap, bad quality rope made in bulk.

These rope makers have proven themselves to be reliable and wonderful, and have on many occasions crafted rope exactly to my specifications:

- HandMade Rope *handmaderope.com*
- Serenity Bound *serenity-bound.com*
- Moco Jute *mocojute.com*
- Knotty Kink *knottykink.com/bondage-rope*
- Madam Butterfly *butterflyrope.com*
- Maui Kink *mauikink.com*
- Aja Rope *ajarope.com*
- Shibari Ropes *shibariropes.com*
- Twisted Monk *twistedmonk.com*
- Kinky Ropes *kinkyropes.com*
- Beautiful Bondage UK *beautifulbondage.net*

Acknowledgments

I could never have accomplished this book without the help of what I consider to be the greatest rigging team in history. The talented individuals in this team have learned to work together as a cohesive unit, succeeding within the confines of being on set and the time restraints that brings with it and being creative and innovative under enormous pressure. All the images you see shot in this book were accomplished over four days, internationally; a massive undertaking.

Allura is a passionate rigger hailing from Toronto, ON and has been practicing rope seriously for four years. First encountering rope bondage and suspension at Subspace fetish parties, they were immediately taken by its beauty and practicality. Through events like Hitchin Bitches and MBE along with studying others' rope on the internet, their skill and passion flourished. They are heavily influenced by Milla Reika, ve-ra and local Toronto riggers as well as their own creativity.

Ruairidh (pronounced roo-ah-ree) is a Toronto-born and bred rope artist who's been interested in bondage since he could tie his own shoes. Over the years he has developed a distinctive style of rope weaving, covering bodies with large-scale rope creations that range from beautifully severe bondage to severely beautiful fashion apparel. Ruairidh draws inspiration for his art from a wide array of sources including nature, old architecture, modern engineering and even haute couture. He has been teaching weaving techniques for several years, at his local and international bondage groups. Find Ruairidh at ruairidh.ca or on FetLife.

ve-ra first discovered her fascination with bondage at MBE in 2008 and since then has had the privilege of working with some of the world's best talent in this arena. Inspired mostly by ballet and contemporary dance, she has used her knowledge of the physical body to create works of art with Japanese-influenced rope. Since having first received lessons through her local community, she has been able to meet and learn from talented rope artists such as Wykd Dave and Clover, Yukimura Haruki and most recently, Kazami Ranki. ve-ra now teaches rope bondage internationally, sharing her love of rope with anyone with the passion to learn the art, and I've been lucky enough to come along on her journey too.

Rone has been studying rope bondage for four years, and in that time it has become one of her largest passions. Rone fell in love with rope the moment ve-ra first tied her, and has developed from being a model in my previous books to being a fantastic rigger in her own right. She cites her influences as Kazami and myself, as well as Osaka Dan who has really showed her the ropes—literally!

Tho4ns (ThoRns) has been practicing rope bondage as well as bondage photography since early 2003. While these are very much a lifelong pursuit for him, his focus is on the more traditional Japanese aspects of rope bondage that are echoed in his tying style. As a rigger his passion remains on bringing to the surface the more engaging and connected aspects of rope bondage. The beauty of bondage, for Tho4ns, revolves around confining the body and freeing the mind and the heart. It is also, however, in the journey of getting there and back and how this sometimes-winding road is interpreted by and through one's partner. This experience is brought to the surface through the complex and creative language of rope. His work has been published in magazines, books and online publications worldwide, including on his own blog at tho4ns.com.

My special thanks go out to Cylr, Osaka Dan and JD of the Toronto Kinbaku Salon. I would also like to thank Blair Devorr, Holly Randall, Tera Patrick and Adventureseeker2 for being an integral part of my work. Makeup and hair by Rosalinda and Cammy, Styling by Mia and AJ from Stylehouse99.

Wardrobe provided by The Stockroom (stockroom.com), Kink Engineering (kinkengineering.com) and NorthBound Leather (northbound.com).

Thanks to *Hustler Hollywood* for their incredible support and their hosting of my regular column (hustlerhollywoodstores.com/author/lord-morpheous/).

Thanks to Mo who is an average guy and Ashes Wednesday who is not so average.

Most of all I would like to thank the models who worked with me during long hours on set to complete this book. I personally selected all of you because of your interest and the passion you have for the craft of rope bondage.

In no particular order: Stevie Shae, Samantha Rone, Alex Chance, Johnny Castle, Vanessa Lake, Sarah Hunter, Celeste Star, Ana Foxxx, Seth Gamble, Jayden James, Odette Delcroix, Kerry Maguire, Blair Devorr, Samantha Saint, Ryan Driller, Aaliyah Love, Spencer Scott, Sophia Jade, Sofia Ferreria, Kylie Maria, Jasmine Love, Casey King, Candle Box, Marie Mcray, Kourtney Kane, Sarah Peachez, Bonnie Rotten, Maddy O'Reilly,

Idelsy Love, Archean, Mosh, Lola Fox and Dani Daniels. You all came together as lovers of rope bondage and have helped to create a beautiful book. It has been an honor working with you.

About the Author

Morpheous is a Canadian sex educator, author, photographer, and kinkster based in New York. This is his third book for Green Candy Press, following on the heels of his popular BDSM books *How to be Kinky: A Beginner's Guide to BDSM* and *How to be Kinkier: More Adventures in Adult Playtime* (2008 / 2012, Green Candy Press, San Francisco) and fourth book overall. Morpheous' work is archived in the Sexual Representation Collection of the University of Toronto's Mark S. Bonham Centre for Sexual Diversity Studies, at the Leather Archives and Museum in Chicago, and at the National Archives of Canada.

Morpheous has taught a variety of workshops on rope bondage, the aesthetics of bondage, fetish photography, advanced and beginner BDSM, and workshops catered to professional Dominants and submissives. He travels and presents regularly, doing outreach to both academic and kink-aware safer sex organizations as well as performing in rope bondage expos the world over.

He is also the founder of Morpheous' Bondage Extravaganza, an annual rope bondage art installation that has grown over the years into the world's largest public rope bondage event, with upwards of 6000 spectators in all the events across cities around the world with 75,000 more watching online. Though the event started as a part of Toronto's annual Nuit Blanche all-night art festival, it expanded to include another MBE nights across the world, including Sydney, Rio de Janeiro, Manila, San Francisco, Cincinnati, Montreal, Vienna, Orlando, Florida and more. Check out mbeworldwide.com.

You can find out more about Morpheous at lordmorpheous.com.